Where I Was From

Where I Was From

Joan Didion

Alfred A. Knopf   New York

2003

THIS IS A BORZOI BOOK
PUBLISHED BY ALFRED A. KNOPF

In progress and in different form, parts of *Where I Was From* appeared
in *The New York Review of Books, Esquire,* and *The New Yorker.*

Library of Congress Cataloging-in-Publication Data
Didion, Joan.
    Where I was from / Joan Didion.—1st ed.
        p. cm.
    ISBN 0-679-43332-5
    1. California—History.   2. California—Social conditions.   3. California—
In literature.   4. National characteristics, American.   I. Title
F861.D53 2003
979.4—dc21   2002043325

Manufactured in the United States of America
Published September 29, 2003
Second Printing, October 2003

This book is for my brother
James Jerrett Didion,
and for our mother and father,
Eduene Jerrett Didion
and
Frank Reese Didion,
with love

Part One

I

MY great-great-great-great-great-grandmother Elizabeth Scott was born in 1766, grew up on the Virginia and Carolina frontiers, at age sixteen married an eighteen-year-old veteran of the Revolution and the Cherokee expeditions named Benjamin Hardin IV, moved with him into Tennessee and Kentucky and died on still another frontier, the Oil Trough Bottom on the south bank of the White River in what is now Arkansas but was then Missouri Territory. Elizabeth Scott Hardin was remembered to have hidden in a cave with her children (there were said to have been eleven, only eight of which got recorded) during Indian fighting, and to have been so strong a swimmer that she could ford a river in flood with an infant in her arms. Either in her defense or for reasons of his own, her husband was said to have killed, not counting English soldiers or Cherokees, ten men. This may be true or it may be, in a local oral tradition inclined to stories that turn on decisive gestures, embroidery. I have it on the word of a cousin who researched the matter that the husband, our great-great-great-great-great-grandfather, "appears in the standard printed histories of Arkansas as 'Old Colonel Ben Hardin, the hero of so many

Indian wars.'" Elizabeth Scott Hardin had bright blue eyes and sick headaches. The White River on which she lived was the same White River on which, a century and a half later, James McDougal would locate his failed White-water development. This is a country at some level not as big as we like to say it is.

I know nothing else about Elizabeth Scott Hardin, but I have her recipe for corn bread, and also for India relish: her granddaughter brought these recipes west in 1846, traveling with the Donner-Reed party as far as the Humboldt Sink before cutting north for Oregon, where her husband, the Reverend Josephus Adamson Cornwall, was determined to be the first Cumberland Presbyterian circuit rider in what was then called Oregon country. Because that granddaughter, Nancy Hardin Cornwall, was my great-great-great-grandmother, I have, besides her recipes, a piece of appliqué she made on the crossing. This appliqué, green and red calico on a muslin field, hangs now in my dining room in New York and hung before that in the living room of a house I had on the Pacific Ocean.

I also have a photograph of the stone marker placed on the site of the cabin in which Nancy Hardin Cornwall and her family spent the winter of 1846–47, still short of their destination in the Willamette Valley but unable to get their wagons through a steep defile on the Umpqua River without abandoning Josephus Cornwall's books. (This option seems to have presented itself only to his daughters.) "Dedicated to the memory of Rev. J. A. Corn-wall and family," the engraving on the marker reads.

"They built the first immigrant cabin in Douglas County near this site, hence the name Cabin Creek. The family wintered here in 1846–1847, were saved from extreme want by Israel Stoley, a nephew who was a good hunter. The Indians were friendly. The Cornwalls traveled part way westward with the ill-fated Donner Party."

My mother was sent the photograph of this marker by her mother's cousin Oliver Huston, a family historian so ardent that as recently as 1957 he was alerting descendants to "an occasion which no heir should miss," the presentation to the Pacific University Museum of, among other artifacts, "the old potato masher which the Cornwall family brought across the plains in 1846." Oliver Huston's letter continued: "By this procedure, such items can then be seen by all Geiger and Cornwall heirs at any time in the future by simply visiting the Museum." I have not myself found occasion to visit the potato masher, but I do have a typescript of certain memories, elicited from one of Nancy Hardin Cornwall's twelve children, Narcissa, of those months on what would later be called Cabin Creek:

We were about ten miles from the Umpqua River and the Indians living there would come and spend the greater part of the day. There was one who spoke English, and he told Mother the Rogue River Indians were coming to kill us. Mother told them if they troubled us, in the spring the Bostons (the Indian name for the white people) would come out and kill them all off. Whether this had any effect or not I don't know, but anyway they did not kill us. But we always thought they would come one day for that purpose. One day Father was busy reading and did not notice the house was filling with strange Indians until Mother spoke about it. . . . As soon as Father noticed them he got up and got his pistols and asked the Indians to go out and see him shoot. They followed him out, but kept at a distance. The pistols were a great curiosity to them. I doubt if they had ever seen any before. As soon as they were all out of the cabin Mother barred the door and would not let them in any more. Father entertained them outside until evening, when they got on their ponies and rode away. They never returned to trouble us any more.

In another room of this house I had on the Pacific Ocean there hung a quilt from another crossing, a quilt made by my great-great-grandmother Elizabeth Anthony Reese on a wagon journey during which she buried one child, gave birth to another, twice contracted mountain fever, and took turns driving a yoke of oxen, a span of mules, and twenty-two head of loose stock. In this quilt of Elizabeth Reese's were more stitches than I had ever seen in a quilt, a blinding and pointless compaction of stitches, and it occurred to me as I hung it that she must have finished it one day in the middle of the crossing, somewhere in the wilderness of her own grief and illness, and just kept on stitching. From her daughter's account:

Tom was sick with fever the first day of the crossing, no chance for a doctor. He was only sick a day or two when he died. He had to be buried right away, as the train of wagons was going right on. He was two years old, and we were glad to get a trunk to bury him in. A friend gave a trunk. My aunt, the following year, when her baby died, carried it for a long time in her arms without letting anyone know for fear they would bury the baby before coming to a station.

These women in my family would seem to have been pragmatic and in their deepest instincts clinically radical, given to breaking clean with everyone and everything they knew. They could shoot and they could handle stock and when their children outgrew their shoes they could learn from the Indians how to make moccasins. "An old lady in our wagon train taught my sister to make blood pudding," Narcissa Cornwall recalled. "After killing a deer or steer you cut its throat and catch the blood. You add suet to this and a little salt, and meal or flour if you have it, and bake it. If you haven't anything else to eat, it's pretty good." They tended to accommodate any means in pursuit of an uncertain end. They tended to avoid dwelling on just what that end might imply. When they could not think what else to do they moved another thousand miles, set out another garden: beans and squash and sweet peas from seeds carried from the last place. The past could be jettisoned, children buried and parents left behind, but seeds got carried. They were women, these women in my family, without much time for second thoughts, without much inclination toward equivocation, and later, when there was time or inclination, there developed a tendency, which I came to see as endemic, toward slight and major derangements, apparently eccentric pronouncements, opaque bewilderment and moves to places not quite on the schedule.

Mother viewed character as being the mainspring of life, and, therefore, as regulating our lives here and indicating our destiny in the life to come. She had fixed and settled principles, aims and motives in life. Her general health was excellent and in middle life she appeared almost incapable of fatigue. Winter and summer, at all seasons and every day, except Sunday, her life was one ceaseless round of activity. The care of her family, to provide for hired help, to entertain visitors, and to entertain preachers and others during meetings which were frequent.

That was the view of Nancy Hardin Cornwall taken by her son Joseph, who was thirteen years old during the crossing. Nancy Hardin Cornwall's daughter Laura, two years old during the crossing, took a not dissimilar view: "Being a Daughter of the American Revolution, she was naturally a brave woman, never seeming afraid of Indians or shrinking from hardships."

A photograph:

A woman standing on a rock in the Sierra Nevada in perhaps 1905.

Actually it is not just a rock but a granite promontory: an igneous outcropping. I use words like "igneous" and "outcropping" because my grandfather, one of whose mining camps can be seen in the background of this photograph, taught me to use them. He also taught me to distinguish gold-bearing ores from the glittering but worthless serpentine I preferred as a child, an education to no point, since by that time gold was no more worth mining than serpentine and the distinction academic, or possibly wishful.

The photograph. The promontory. The camp in the background.

And the woman: Edna Magee Jerrett. She is Nancy Hardin Cornwall's great-granddaughter, she will in time be my grandmother. She is Black Irish, English, Welsh, possibly (this is uncertain) a fraction Jewish through her grandfather William Geiger, who liked to claim as an ancestor a German rabbi but was himself a Presbyterian missionary in the Sandwich Islands and along the Pacific coast; possibly (this is still more uncertain) a lesser fraction Indian, from some frontier somewhere, or maybe, because her skin darkens in the sun as she was told not to let it, she just likes to say that. She grew up in a house on the Oregon coast filled with the educational curiosities of the place and period: strings of shells and seeds from Tahiti, carved emu eggs, Satsuma vases, spears from the

South Pacific, an alabaster miniature of the Taj Mahal and the baskets her mother was given by the local Indians. She is quite beautiful. She is also quite indulged, clearly given, although she knows enough about mountains to shake out her boots for snakes every morning, to more amenities than could have been offered in this mining camp in the Sierra Nevada at the time in question. In this photograph she is wearing, for example, a long suede skirt and jacket made for her by the most expensive tailor in San Francisco. "You couldn't pay for her *hats*," her father, a ship's captain, had told her suitors by way of discouragement, and perhaps they had all been discouraged but my grandfather, an innocent from the Georgetown Divide who read books.

It was an extravagance of spirit that would persist through her life. Herself a child, she knew what children wanted. When I was six and had the mumps she brought me, as solace, not a coloring book, not ice cream, not bubble bath, but an ounce of expensive perfume, Elizabeth Arden "On Dit," in a crystal bottle sealed with gold thread. When I was eleven and declined to go any longer to church she gave me, as inducement, not the fear of God but a hat, not any hat, not a child's well-mannered cloche or beret, but a *hat,* gossamer Italian straw and French silk cornflowers and a heavy satin label that read "Lilly Dache." She made champagne punch for the grandchildren left to sit with her on New Year's Eve. During World War II she volunteered to help salvage the Central Valley tomato crop by working the line at the Del Monte cannery in Sacramento, took one look at the moving conveyer belt, got one of those sick headaches her great-grandmother brought west with the seeds, and spent that first and only day on the line with tears running down her face. As atonement, she spent the rest of the war knitting socks for the Red Cross to send to the front. The yarn she bought to knit these socks was cashmere, in regulation colors. She had vicuña coats, hand-milled soap, and not much money. A child could make her cry, and I am ashamed to say that I sometimes did.

She was bewildered by many of the events in her adult life. One of her seafaring brothers became unstable when his ship hit a mine crossing the Atlantic; the son of another committed suicide. She witnessed the abrupt slide into madness of her only sister. Raised to believe that her life would be, as her great-grandmother's was said to have been, one ceaseless round of fixed and settled principles, aims, motives, and activity, she could sometimes think of nothing to do but walk downtown, check out the Bon Marché for clothes she could not afford, buy a cracked crab for dinner and take a taxi home. She died when I was twenty-three and I have of hers a petit-point evening bag, two watercolors she painted as a young girl in an Episcopal convent school (the watermelon still life, the mission she had never seen at San Juan Capistrano), twelve butter knives she had made at Shreve's in San Francisco, and fifty shares of Transamerica stock. I was instructed by her will to sell the stock for something I wanted and could not afford. "What will she have to look forward to," my mother scolded my grandmother on the occasions of the ounce of "On Dit," the Lilly Daché hat, the black scarf embroidered with jet to assuage the pain of dancing school. In the generational theater my mother, despite what I came to recognize as a recklessness quite outside my grandmother's range, had been assigned the role described in the stage directions as sensible. "She'll find something," my grandmother always said, a reassuring conclusion if not one entirely supported by her own experience.

A nother photograph, another grandmother: Ethel Reese Didion, who I never knew. She caught fever during the waning days of the 1918 influenza epidemic and died, leaving a husband and two small boys, one of them my father, on the morning of the false armistice. Many times my father told me that she died thinking the war was over. He told me this each time as if it were a matter of considerable importance, and perhaps it was, since on reflection that is all he ever told me about what she thought on any subject. My great-aunt Nell, her younger sister, would say only that my grandmother had been "nervous," and "different." Different from what, I used to ask. Aunt Nell would light another cigarette, consign it immediately to a heavy quartz ashtray, and slide her big rings up and down her thin fingers. Ethel was nervous, she would finally repeat. You could never tease Ethel. Ethel was, well, different.

In this photograph, taken in about 1904, Ethel is at a Grange picnic in Florin, at that time a farm settlement south of Sacramento. She has not yet married the man, my grandfather, whose startling taciturnity would remain so inexplicable to her family, the man to whom I sometimes referred as "Grandfather Didion" but never addressed directly, from the time I was a small child until the day he died in 1953, by any form more familiar than "Mr. Didion." She is still Ethel Reese in this picture and she is wearing a white shirtwaist and a straw hat. Her brothers and cousins, ranchers' sons with a bent for good times and a gift for losing things without rancor, laugh at something outside the camera's range. Aunt Nell, the smallest, darts among their legs. My grandmother smiles tentatively. Her eyes are shut against the sun, or against the camera. I was said to have her eyes, "Reese eyes," eyes that reddened and watered at the first premonition of sun or primroses or raised voices, and I was also said to have some of her "difference," her way of being less than easy at that moment when the dancing starts, but there would be no way of knowing any of that from this picture of Ethel Reese at the Florin Grange picnic in about 1904. This is the memory of her aunt, Catherine Reese, a child during the Reese family's 1852 crossing, of the last stage and aftermath of the journey during which her mother made the quilt with the blinding compaction of stitches:

> Came by Carson City climbing mountains all the time, to Lake Tahoe and on down. Lived in the mountains as Father was sick with chills and fever. Had to give up our stock driver and Mother looked after the stock. Found two or three families of old country folk and lived with them until we

got located in a sheep herder's house and lived the
winter with him until Father got a house built on
the hill ranch near Florin, $2 an acre government
land. Father paid cash for 360 acres as he had sold
the team and had some money. Went to raising
grain and stock, had twelve cows and made and
sold butter and eggs and chickens, once in a while
a calf. Drove to Sacramento once a week to sell the
stuff. Father and Dave did the churning, Mother
and I did the milking. I walked six miles to
school, to where the graveyard is now on Stockton
Boulevard.

That first Reese ranch in Florin, enlarged after a few
years from 360 to 640 acres, was into my adult life still
owned by my family, or, more precisely, by a corporation
called the Elizabeth Reese Estate Company, the sharehold-
ers in which were all members of my family. Occasionally,
late at night, my father and brother and I would talk
about buying out the interests of our cousins in what we
still called "the hill ranch" (there was no actual "hill," but
there was on the original acreage a rise of perhaps a foot), a
move that would have pleased them, since most of them
wanted to sell it. I was never able to ascertain whether my
father's interest in holding this particular ranch was in any
way sentimental; he spoke of it only as a cold property in
the short term but a potentially hot one in the long. My
mother had no interest in keeping the hill ranch, or in fact
any California land: California, she said, was now too reg-
ulated, too taxed, too expensive. She spoke enthusiasti-

cally, on the other hand, about moving to the Australian outback.

"Eduene," my father would say, a remonstration.

"I would," she would insist, reckless.

"Just leave California? Give it all up?"

"In a *minute*," she would say, the pure strain talking, Elizabeth Scott's great-great-great-great-granddaughter. "Just *forget* it."

2

"ONE hundred years ago, our great-great-grand-parents were pushing America's frontier west-ward, to California." So began the speech I wrote to deliver at my eighth-grade graduation from the Arden School, outside Sacramento. The subject was "Our California Heritage." Developing a theme encouraged by my mother and grandfather, I continued, made rather more confident than I should have been by the fact that I was wearing a new dress, pale green organdy, and my mother's crystal necklace:

> They who came to California were not the self-satisfied, happy and content people, but the adventurous, the restless, and the daring. They were different even from those who settled in other western states. They didn't come west for homes and security, but for adventure and money. They pushed in over the mountains and founded the biggest cities in the west. Up in the Mother Lode they mined gold by day and danced by night. San Francisco's population multiplied almost twenty times, until 1906, when it burned

to the ground, and was built up again nearly as quickly as it had burned. We had an irrigation problem, so we built the greatest dams the world has known. Now both desert and valley are producing food in enormous quantities. California has accomplished much in the past years. It would be easy for us to sit back and enjoy the results of the past. But we can't do this. We can't stop and become satisfied and content. We must live up to our heritage, go on to better and greater things for California.

That was June 1948.

The pale green of the organdy dress was a color that existed in the local landscape only for the few spring days when the rice first showed.

The crystal necklace was considered by my mother an effective way to counter the Valley heat.

Such was the blinkering effect of the local dreamtime that it would be some years before I recognized that certain aspects of "Our California Heritage" did not add up, starting with but by no means limited to the fact that I had delivered it to an audience of children and parents who had for the most part arrived in California during the 1930s, refugees from the Dust Bowl. It was after this realization that I began trying to find the "point" of California, to locate some message in its history. I picked up a book of revisionist studies on the subject, but abandoned it on discovering that I was myself quoted, twice. You will have perhaps realized by now (a good deal earlier than I myself realized) that this book represents an exploration into my own confusions about the place and the way in which I grew up, confusions as much about America as about California, misapprehensions and misunderstandings so much a part of who I became that I can still to this day confront them only obliquely.

3

A GOOD deal about California does not, on its own preferred terms, add up. The Sacramento River, the main source of surface water in a state where distrust of centralized governmental authority has historically passed for an ethic, has its headwaters in the far northern ranges of Siskiyou County. It picks up the waters of the McCloud and the Pit Rivers above Redding, of the Feather and the Yuba and the Bear below Knight's Landing, of the American at Sacramento, of the San Joaquin below Steamboat Slough; and empties through San Francisco Bay into the Pacific, draining the deep snowpacks of the southern Cascades and the northern Sierra Nevada. "The river here is about 400 yards wide," one of my great-great-grandfathers, William Kilgore, whose daughter Myra married into the Reese family, wrote in the journal of his arrival in Sacramento in August of 1850. "The tide raises the water about 2 ft. and steamboats and vessels are here daily. From this place to San Francisco is about 150 miles by water. All of this distance the river has low banks and is subject to inundation for several miles back." That the land to which he intended eventually to bring his wife and two children was "subject to inundation for several miles back" seems not to have presented itself as an argument against immediate settlement. "This is one of the trying mornings for me, as I now have to leave my family, or back out," he had written in his journal four months before. "Suffice it to say, we started." Yet this river that had been from the beginning his destination was one regularly and predictably given, during all but the driest of those years before its flow was controlled or rearranged, to turning its valley into a shallow freshwater sea a hundred miles long and as wide as the distance between the coast ranges and the foothills of the Sierra Nevada: a pattern of flooding, the Army Corps of Engineers declared in 1927, more intense and intractable than that on any other American river system including the Mississippi.

This annual reappearance of a marsh that did not drain to the sea until late spring or summer was referred to locally not as flooding but as "the high water," a seasonal fact of life, no more than an inconvenient but minor cost of the rich bottom land it created, and houses were routinely built with raised floors to accommodate it. Many Sacramento houses during my childhood had on their walls one or another lithograph showing the familiar downtown grid with streets of water, through which citizens could be seen going about their business by raft or rowboat. Some of these lithographs pictured the high water of 1850, after which a three-foot earthen levee between the river and the settlement was built. Others showed the high water of 1852, during which that first levee was washed out. Still others showed the high water of 1853 or 1860 or 1861 or 1862, nothing much changing except the increasing number of structures visible on the grid. "If you will take, on a map of California, Stockton, Sacramento, and San Francisco as guiding points, you will see that a large part of the land lying between these cities is marked 'swamp and overflowed,'" Charles Nordhoff, the grandfather of the co-author of *Mutiny on the Bounty,* wrote in his 1874 *Northern California, Oregon and the Sandwich Islands:*

Until within five or six years these lands attracted but little attention. It was known that they were extremely fertile, but it was thought that the cost and uncertainty of reclaiming them were too great to warrant the enterprise. Of late, however, they have been rapidly bought up by capitalists, and their sagacity has been justified by the results on those tracts which have been reclaimed. These Tule lands . . . are simply deposits of muck, a mixture of the wash or sediment brought down by the Sacramento and San Joaquin rivers with the decayed vegetable matter resulting from an immense growth of various grasses, and of the reed called the "tule," which often grows ten feet high in a season, and decays every year. . . . The swamp and overflowed lands were given by Congress to the State, and the State has, in its turn, virtually given them to private persons. It has sold them for one dollar per acre, of which twenty percent was paid down, or twenty cents per acre; and this money, less some small charges for recording the transfer and for inspecting the reclamation, is returned by the State to the purchaser if he, within three years after the purchase, reclaims his land. That is to say, the State gives away the land on condition that it shall be reclaimed and brought into cultivation.

The creation of the entirely artificial environment that is now the Sacramento Valley was not achieved at one stroke, nor is it complete to this day. Bulletins on when and where the rivers would crest, on the conditions of levees and the addresses of evacuation centers, remained into my adult life the spring commonplaces of Sacramento life, as did rumors that one or another levee had been (or was being, or would be) covertly dynamited by one or another agency looking to save one or another downstream community. During years when repeated storms rolling in from the Pacific coincide with an early melting of the Sierra snowpack, levees still break, sections of interstate highways get destabilized by the rising water table, and the big dams go to crisis mode, trying to save themselves by releasing water as they get it, unchecked, no control, the runoff from the pack running free to the sea.

Reclamation of the tule lands has been a war, for those waging it, in which no armament could be too costly, no strategy too quixotic. By 1979, when the State of California published William L. Kahrl's *The California Water Atlas,* there were 980 miles of levee, 438 miles of canal. There were fifty miles of collecting canals and seepage ditches. There were three drainage pumping plants, five low-water check dams, thirty-one bridges, ninety-one gauging stations, and eight automatic shortwave water-stage transmitters. There were seven weirs opening onto seven bypasses covering 101,000 acres. There were not only the big headwater dams, Shasta on the Sacramento and Folsom on the American and Oroville on the Feather, but all their predecessors and collateral dams, their after-bays and forebays and diversions: Thermalito and Lake Almanor and Frenchman Lake and Little Grass Valley on the Feather, New Bullard's Bar and Englebright and Jackson Meadows and Lake Spaulding on the Yuba, Camp Far West and Rollins and Lower Bear on the Bear, Nimbus and Slab Creek and L. L. Anderson on the American, Box Canyon and Keswick on the Sacramento. The cost of controlling or rearranging the Sacramento, which is to say the "reclamation" of the Sacramento Valley, was largely borne, like the cost of controlling or rearranging many other inconvenient features of California life, by the federal government.

This extreme reliance of California on federal money, so seemingly at odds with the emphasis on unfettered individualism that constitutes the local core belief, was a pattern set early on, and derived in part from the very individualism it would seem to belie. ("They didn't come west for homes and security, but for adventure and money," as "Our California Heritage" put it.) Charles Nordhoff complained of California in 1874 that "a speculative spirit invades even the farm-house," too often tempting its citizens "to go from one avocation to another, to do many things superficially, and to look for sudden fortunes by the chances of a shrewd venture, rather than be content to live by patient and continued labor." There had been from the beginning virtually no notion of "pushing America's frontier westward," my eighth-grade conception of it notwithstanding: the American traders and trappers who began settling in California as early as 1826 were leaving their own country for a remote Mexican province, Alta California. Many became naturalized Mexican citizens. Many married into Mexican and Spanish families. A fair number received grants of land from the Mexican authorities. As late as 1846, American emigrants were starting west with the idea of reaching territory at least provisionally Mexican, only to find on their arrival that the Bear Flag Revolt and the Mexican War had placed Alta California under American military authority. There it would remain—along with the other American spoil of that conquest, the territory that eventually became Nevada and Utah and New Mexico and Arizona and part of Colorado—until California was admitted to the union as a state in 1850.

Predicated as it was on this general notion of cutting loose and striking it rich, the California settlement had tended to attract drifters of loosely entrepreneurial inclination, the hunter-gatherers of the frontier rather than its cultivators, and to reward most fully those who perceived most quickly that the richest claim of all lay not in the minefields but in Washington. It was a quartet of Sacramento shopkeepers, Charles Crocker and Leland Stanford and Collis P. Huntington and Mark Hopkins, who built the railroad that linked California with the world markets and opened the state to extensive settlement, but it was the citizens of the rest of the country who paid for it, through a federal cash subsidy (sixteen thousand dollars a mile in the valley and forty-eight thousand dollars a mile in the "mountains," which were contractually defined as beginning six miles east of Sacramento) plus a federal land grant, ten or twenty checkerboarded square-mile sections, for each mile of track laid.

Nor did the role of the government stop with the construction of the railroad: the citizens of the rest of the country would also, in time, subsidize the crops the railroad carried, make possible the irrigation of millions of acres of essentially arid land, underwrite the rhythms of planting and not planting, and create, finally, a vast agricultural mechanism in a kind of market vacuum, quite remote from the normal necessity for measuring supply against demand and cost against return. As recently as 1993, eighty-two thousand acres in California were still planted in alfalfa, a low-value crop requiring more water than was then used in the households of all thirty million Californians. Almost a million and a half acres were planted in cotton, the state's second largest consumer of water, a crop subsidized directly by the federal government. Four hundred thousand acres were planted in rice, the cultivation of which involves submerging the fields under six inches of water from mid-April until the August harvest, months during which, in California, no rain falls. The 1.6 million acre feet of water this required (an acre foot is roughly 326,000 gallons) was made available, even in drought years, for what amounted to a nominal subsidized price by the California State Water Project and the Central Valley Project, an agency of the federal government, which, through the commodity-support program of the Department of Agriculture, also subsidized the crop itself. Ninety percent of this California rice was glutinous medium-grain Japonica, a type not popular in the United States but favored in both Japan and Korea, each of which banned the import of California rice. These are the kinds of contradictions on which Californians have tended to founder when they try to think about the place they come from.

4

JOSIAH ROYCE, who was from 1885 until his death in 1916 a central figure in what later became known as the "golden period" of the Harvard philosophy department, was born in Grass Valley, not far from Sacramento, grew up there and in San Francisco, and in some sense spent the rest of his life trying to make coherent the discontinuities implicit in this inheritance. "My native town was a mining town in the Sierra Nevada—a place five or six years older than myself," he said at a dinner given in his honor at the Walton Hotel in Philadelphia in 1915.

My earliest recollections include a very frequent wonder as to what my elders meant when they said that this was a new community. I frequently looked at the vestiges left by the former diggings of miners, saw that many pine logs were rotten, and that a miner's grave was to be found in a lonely place not far from my own house. Plainly men had lived and died thereabouts. I dimly reflected that this sort of life had apparently been going on ever since men dwelt thereabouts. The logs and the grave looked old. The sunsets were beautiful. The wide prospects when one looked across the Sacramento Valley were impressive, and had long interested the people of whose love for my country I heard so much. What was there then in this place that ought to be called new, or for that matter crude? I wondered, and gradually came to feel that part of my life's business was to find out what all this wonder meant.

Here we come close to a peculiar California confusion: what Royce had actually made it his "life's business" to do, his work, did not resolve "what all this wonder meant." Instead, Royce invented an idealized California, an ethical system in which "loyalty" was the basic virtue, the moral law essential to the creation of "community," which was in turn man's only salvation and by extension the redeeming essence of the California settlement. Yet the California community most deeply recalled by the author of this system was what he acknowledged to have been "a community of irresponsible strangers" (or, in another reference, "a blind and stupid and homeless generation of selfish wanderers"), a community not of the "loyal" but of "men who have left homes and families, who have fled from before the word of the Lord, and have sought safety from their old vexatious duties in a golden paradise."

Such calls to dwell upon the place and its meaning (and, if the meaning proved intractable, to reinvent the place) had been general in California since the first American settlement, the very remoteness of which was sufficiently extreme to raise questions about why one was there, why one had come there, what the voyage would ultimately mean. The overland crossing itself had an aspect of quest: "One was going on a pilgrimage whose every suggestion was of the familiar sacred stories," Royce wrote. "One sought a romantic and far-off golden land of promise, and one was in the wilderness of this world, often guided only by signs from heaven. . . . The clear blue was almost perpetually overhead; the pure mountain winds were about one; and again, even in the hot and parched deserts, a mysterious power provided the few precious springs and streams of water."

Each arriving traveler had been, by definition, reborn in the wilderness, a new creature in no way the same as the man or woman or even child who had left Independence or St. Joseph however many months before: the very decision to set forth on the journey had been a kind of death, involving the total abandonment of all previous life, mothers and fathers and brothers and sisters who would never again be seen, all sentiment banished, the most elementary comforts necessarily relinquished. "I had for months anticipated this hour, yet, not till it came, did I realize the blank dreariness of seeing night come on without house or home to shelter us and our baby-girl," Josiah Royce's mother, Sarah, wrote of the day in 1849 on which she set off for Sacramento with her husband and first child.

The blank dreariness, Sarah Royce wrote.

Without house or home, Sarah Royce wrote.

Suffice it to say, we started, my great-great-grandfather William Kilgore wrote.

This moment of leaving, the death that must precede the rebirth, is a fixed element of the crossing story. Such stories are artlessly told. There survives in their repetition a problematic elision or inflation, a narrative flaw, a problem with point of view: the actual observer, or camera eye, is often hard to locate. This was Josephus Adamson Cornwall's goodbye to his mother, as related by a son who seems to have heard the story from his mother, Nancy Hardin Cornwall, she of the fixed and settled principles, aims, and motives in life, who had not herself been present: "Just ready to go, he entered his mother's parlor. She went out with him to his horse to say the last words and to see him depart. She told him that she would never again see him in this world, gave him her blessing, and commended him to God. He then mounted his horse and rode away, while she followed him with a last look, until he vanished from sight."

Who witnessed this moment of departure? Was the camera on Josephus Cornwall's mother, following her son with the last look? Or on the son himself, glancing back as he vanishes from sight? The gravity of the decisive break demands narrative. Conflicting details must be resolved, reworked into a plausible whole. Aging memories will be recorded as gospel. Children recount as the given of their personal and cultural history what neither they nor even their parents could possibly have known, for example the "providential interposition" that was said to have saved

Josephus Cornwall's life when he was an infant in Georgia: "It was a peculiarity of that section of the state that mad dogs were very common. One day when his parents were busy he was left in the house alone in his cradle. A mad dog entered the room, walked around it and went away, but never molested him." What witness saw the mad dog enter the room? Did the witness take action, or merely observe and report, trusting the "providential interposition" to save the baby?

Yet it was through generations of just such apparently omniscient narrators that the crossing stories became elevated to a kind of single master odyssey, its stations of veneration fixed. There were the Platte, the Sandy, the Big and Little Sandys. There was the Green River. Fort Hall. Independence Rock. The Sweetwater. There were the Humboldt, the Humboldt Sink, the Hastings cut-off. The names were so deeply embedded in the stories I heard as a child that when I happened at age twenty to see the Green River, through the windows of a train crossing Wyoming, I was astonished by this apparent evidence that it actually existed, a fact on the ground, there to be seen—entirely unearned—by anyone passing by. Just as there were stations of veneration, so there were objects of veneration, relics of those who had made the redeeming journey. "The old potato masher which the Cornwall family brought across the plains in 1846" was not the only family totem given by my grandmother's cousins to the Pacific University Museum in 1957. "After consulting with certain of the heirs," Oliver Huston wrote, the cousins had also determined "that it will be advisable to turn over to the Museum at that time the small desk sent Grandfather in 1840 by William Johnson from Hawaii, and also certain mementoes of Grandmother Geiger," specifically "the blouse which formed part of her wedding costume" and "the old shawl or shoulder wrap she wore in her later years." So Saxon Brown, the heroine of Jack London's curious "California" novel *The Valley of the Moon,* could hold in her hands her mother's red satin corset ("the pioneer finery of a frontier woman who had crossed the plains") and see pass before her, "from East to West, across a continent, the great hegira of the land-hungry Anglo-Saxon. It was part and fiber of her. She had been nursed on its traditions and its facts from the lips of those who had taken part."

As repeated, this was an odyssey the most important aspect of which was that it offered moral or spiritual "tests," or challenges, with fatal consequences for failure. Josiah Royce's parents, traveling with only their two-year-old daughter, three other emigrants, and a manuscript list of landmarks that stopped at the Humboldt Sink, found themselves lost on the Carson desert, "confused, almost stupefied," "dazed," "half-senseless," suffering for a period "the same fatal horror of desolation and death that had assailed the Donner Party in the Truckee pass." Children who died of cholera got buried on the trail. Women who believed they could keep some token of their mother's house (the rosewood chest, the flat silver) learned to jetti-son memory and keep moving. Sentiment, like grief and dissent, cost time. A hesitation, a moment spent looking back, and the grail was forfeited. Independence Rock, west of Fort Laramie on the Sweetwater River, was so named because the traveler who had not reached that point by the Fourth of July, Independence Day, would not reach the Sierra Nevada before snow closed the passes.

The diaries of emigrants refer to the Sierra Nevada as "the most dreaded moment," "the Great Bugaboo," the source of "sleepless nights," "disturbed dreams." *Without house or home:* Sarah Royce and her husband and child abandoned their wagon and made it through the Sierra, with the help of a United States Army relief party, only ten days before the passes closed. Even while the passes remained open, there would be snow. There would be the repeated need to ford and again ford the Truckee or the Carson. There would be the repeated need to unload and reload the wagons. There would be recent graves, wrecked wagons, and, at Donner Lake, after the winter of 1846–47, human as well as animal bones, and the trees notched to show the depth of the fatal winter's snowpack. This is the entry in William Kilgore's diary for August 1, 1852:

> Ice and frost this morning. Four miles to Red Lake. This is . . . the head of Salmon Trout, or Carson River. It is a small lake and is within one mi. of the summit of the Sierra Nevada. From this lake to the summit the ascent is very great, some places being almost perpendicular. . . . Four mi. from the summit we cross a small creek, a tributary of the Sacramento. . . . At this creek we stop to noon. Here we help inter a young man who

died last night of bilious fever. He was from
Michigan. His name was Joseph Ricker. His parents reside in the state of Maine. Here we ascend
another ridge of this mt. It is higher than the one
we have just passed, being 9,339 ft. above the sea.
From the foot to the summit it is five miles, and in
ascending and descending we travel over four
miles of snow, and it from two to 20 ft. deep. . . .
21 miles today.

To read these crossing accounts and diaries is to be
struck by the regularity with which a certain apprehension of darkness enters the quest, a shadow of moral ambiguity that becomes steadily more pervasive until that
moment when the traveler realizes that the worst of the
Sierra is behind him. "The Summit is crossed!" one such
diary reads. "We are in California! Far away in the haze
the dim outlines of the Sacramento Valley are discernible!
We are on the down grade now and our famished animals
may pull us through. We are in the midst of huge pines,
so large as to challenge belief. Hutton is dead. Others
are worse. I am better." By this point, in every such journey, there would have been the accidents, the broken
bones, the infected and even the amputated hands and
feet. There would have been the fevers. Sarah Royce
remembered staying awake all night after a man in her
party died of cholera, and hearing the wind whip his
winding sheet like "some vindictive creature struggling
restlessly in bonds." There would have been the hurried
burials, in graves often unmarked and sometimes deliber-

ately obliterated. "Before leaving the Humboldt River there was one death, Miss Mary Campbell," Nancy Hardin Cornwall's son Joseph recalled. "She was buried right in our road and the whole train of wagons was driven over her grave to conceal it from the Indians. Miss Campbell died of mountain fever, and Mother by waiting on her caught the fever and for a long time she lingered, apparently between life and death, but at last recovered. Miss Campbell was an orphan, her mother having died at Green River."

There would have been, darkest of all, the betrayals, the suggestions that the crossing might not after all be a noble odyssey, might instead be a mean scrambling for survival, a blind flight on the part of Josiah Royce's "blind and stupid and homeless generation of selfish wanderers." Not all emigrants, to take just one example, cared for all orphans. It was on the Little Sandy that an emigrant named Bernard J. Reid, who had put down two hundred dollars to secure a place on an 1849 crossing, saw first "an emigrant wagon apparently abandoned by its owners" and then "a rude head-board indicating a new grave," which turned out to be that of the Reverend Robert Gilmore and his wife Mary, who had died the same day of cholera. This account comes to us from Reid's diary, which was found by his family in the 1950s, entrusted to Mary McDougall Gordon for editing, and published in 1983 by the Stanford University Press as *Overland to California with the Pioneer Line.* On turning from the grave to the apparently abandoned wagon, Reid tells us, he was "surprised to see a neatly dressed girl of about 17, sitting on the wagon tongue, her feet resting on the grass, and her eyes apparently directed at vacancy."

She seemed like one dazed or in a dream and did not seem to notice me till I spoke to her. I then learned from her in reply to my questions that she was Miss Gilmore, whose parents had died two days before; that her brother, younger than herself, was sick in the wagon, probably with cholera; that their oxen were lost or stolen by the Indians; and that the train they had been traveling with, after waiting for three days on account of the sickness and death of her parents, had gone on that morning, fearful, if they delayed longer, of being caught by winter in the Sierra Nevada mountains. . . . The people of her train had told her that probably her oxen would yet be found, or at any rate some other train coming along with oxen to spare would take her and her brother and their wagon along.

"Who could tell the deep sense of bereavement, distress and desolation that weighed on that poor girl's heart, there in the wilderness with no telling what fate was in store for her and her sick brother?" Reid asks his readers and surely also himself. Such memories might have seemed difficult to reconcile with the conviction that one had successfully met the tests or challenges required to enter the new life. The redemptive power of the crossing was, nonetheless, the fixed idea of the California settlement, and one that raised a further question: for what exactly, and at what cost, had one been redeemed? When you jettison others so as not to be "caught by winter in the Sierra Nevada mountains," do you deserve not to be caught? When you survive at the cost of Miss Gilmore and her brother, do you survive at all?

5

I WAS born in Sacramento, and lived in California most of my life. I learned to swim in the Sacramento and the American, before the dams. I learned to drive on the levees up and downriver from Sacramento. Yet California has remained in some way impenetrable to me, a wearying enigma, as it has to many of us who are from there. We worry it, correct and revise it, try and fail to define our relationship to it and its relationship to the rest of the country. We make declamatory breaks with it, as Josiah Royce did when he left Berkeley for Harvard. "There is no philosophy in California—from Siskiyou to Ft. Yuma, and from the Golden Gate to the summit of the Sierras," he had written to William James, who eventually responded to this *cri de coeur* with the offer from Harvard. We make equally declamatory returns, as Frank Norris did, determined before his thirtieth birthday "to do some great work with the West and California as a background, and which will be at the same time thoroughly American." The intention, Norris wrote to William Dean Howells, who had reviewed *McTeague* favorably, was "to write three novels around the one subject of *Wheat.* First, a story of California (the producer), second, a story of Chicago (the distributor), third, a story of Europe (the consumer) and in each to keep the idea of this huge Niagara of wheat rolling from West to East. I think a big Epic trilogy could be made out of such a subject, that at the same time would be modern and thoroughly American. The idea is so big that it frightens me at times but I have about made up my mind to have a try at it."

Frank Norris's experience with his subject appears to have been exclusively literary. He was raised in Chicago and then San Francisco, where he met the young woman he would eventually marry at a debutante dance. He spent a year in Paris, studying art and writing a medieval romance, *Yvernelle, A Tale of Feudal France,* which his mother arranged to have published. He spent four years at Berkeley without taking the courses necessary for a degree, then a year as a non-degree student at Harvard. He covered the prelude to the Boer War for *Collier's* and *The San Francisco Chronicle,* the Santiago campaign in Cuba for *McClure's.* At the time he was seized by the trilogy-of-wheat notion, he was living in New York, at 61 Washington Square South.

The Octopus, published in 1901 and based on what was at the time quite recent history in the San Joaquin Valley, was, in the best sense, worked up: through well-situated friends, Ernest Peixotto and his wife (the Peixottos were a prominent San Francisco Jewish family, and Ernest Peixotto's older sister Jessica, an economist, was one of the first women on the faculty of the University of California),

Norris managed an introduction to a couple who ran five thousand acres of wheat in San Benito County, and arranged to spend the summer of 1899 on their ranch near Hollister. San Benito County presented a gentler, more coastal landscape than the San Joaquin, which was where Norris intended to set his novel ("San Juan de Guadala-jara," the mission in *The Octopus,* was a borrow from Mission San Juan Bautista near Hollister, there being no missions in the San Joaquin), but it was nonetheless a setting in which an attentive reporter could absorb the mechanics of a big wheat operation.

The Octopus opens on a day in "the last half of September, the very end of the dry season," a day when "all Tulare County, all the vast reaches of the San Joaquin Valley—in fact all South Central California, was bone dry, parched, and baked and crisped after four months of cloudless weather, when the day seemed always at noon, and the sun blazed white hot over the valley from the Coast Range in the west to the foothills of the Sierras in the east." The stuff of the novel, the incidents on which the narrative turns, came directly from actual events in what was then Tulare County. In 1893 in Tulare County there had been the killing by a sheriff's posse of John Sontag, an embittered Southern Pacific brakeman who had spent the previous three years dynamiting track and robbing trains, killing and wounding several lawmen. In *The Octopus* Sontag would become "Dyke," who commandeers an engineer to escape his pursuers, foils their attempt to derail him by reversing the engine, abandons it, and is taken by the posse.

Thirteen years before, in 1880, there had beer
place then called Mussel Slough but after the in
renamed "Lucerne," the shootout between federal
shals acting for the Southern Pacific, which had be
through its federal land grants the largest landowr
California, and a group of local ranchers who were g
ing wheat on land leased from the railroad. The rand
under the rather willful misapprehension that their
agreements gave them the right to buy the land at $
an acre (the agreements were vaguely worded, but
clearly stated that the land would be made available
various figures from $2.50 upward per acre," "upw
being the word the ranchers preferred to miss), refuse
pay the price, $17 to $40 an acre, ultimately set on
land. The railroad obtained eviction orders, the rancl
resisted, and both the ranchers and the federal marsl
sent to evict them began firing. Six ranchers ultimat
died in this confrontation, which not only provided
climactic incident for *The Octopus*—the showdo
between eleven ranchers and the U.S. marshals sent in
enforce eviction orders—but also influenced the fir
scenes in Josiah Royce's only work of fiction, *The Feud*
Oakfield Creek: A Novel of California Life, based on t
Sacramento squatters' riots of 1850.

For the San Francisco threads in his narrative, Nori
drew on even more recent events: in 1899, there had bee
the celebrated publication in *The San Francisco Examiner*
Edwin Markham's "The Man with the Hoe," a rhetorica
poem that decried the exploitation of labor. An epic poen
in the style of "The Man with the Hoe" appears in *Th*

Octopus as "The Toilers," the newspaper poem that makes an instant celebrity of its author, Presley, the irresolute graduate of "an Eastern college" who is the novel's protagonist. The publication of "The Toilers" enables Presley to dine at the table of "the Railroad King" (Blue Point oysters, *purée a la Derby,* ortolan patties, *grenadins* of bass and stuffed salmon, Londonderry pheasants, *escalopes* of duck, *rissolettes á la pompadour,* asparagus rushed to the kitchen of the Railroad King by special train within hours of its cutting), even as, outside in the fog, the dispossessed widow of one of the evicted and killed San Joaquin wheat growers is literally starving to death, falling into her terminal coma on a vacant lot at the top of the Clay Street hill, her small daughter at her side, her older daughter already descended into prostitution.

Presley knows nothing of the fate of the widow, but had by fortuitous narrative design run into the older daughter, her degradation apparent, that very afternoon, rendering this dinner an occasion for him of considerable clarity. He sits at the opulent table of the Railroad King as the Château Latour is poured and imagines the clink of the glasses "drowned in the explosion of revolvers" in the San Joaquin Valley. He sees, for an instant, "that splendid house sacked to its foundations, the tables overturned, the pictures torn, the hangings blazing, and Liberty, the red-handed Man in the Street, grimed with powder smoke, foul with the gutter, rush yelling, torch in hand, through every door." The intercutting from the dinner table inside to the dying widow and child outside is insistently allegorical, operatic, outsized, as is the subsequent death of

the railroad's agent in the hold of a cargo ship taking on wheat destined for Asia, consigned there by the blind force of the market even as widows and orphans starve for want of a heel of bread on the streets of San Francisco:

> Deafened with the roar of the grain, blinded and made dumb with its chaff, he threw himself forward with clutching fingers, rolling upon his back, and lay there, moving feebly, the head rolling from side to side. The Wheat, leaping continuously from the chute, poured around him. It filled the pockets of the coat, it crept up the sleeves and trouser legs, it covered the great, protuberant stomach, it ran at last in rivulets into the distended, gasping mouth. It covered the face.
>
> Upon the surface of the Wheat, under the chute, nothing moved but the Wheat itself. There was no sign of life. Then, for an instant, the surface stirred. A hand, fat, with short fingers and swollen veins, reached up, clutching, then fell limp and prone. In another instant it was covered.

The Octopus has been, from the outset, a troubling work, in part because its apparent relentlessness could be so readily dismissed. As recently as 1991, in a discussion of the railroad's role in the development of California, the quarterly publication of the California Historical Society was trying to separate the significance of that role from Norris's "shrill, anti-corporate rhetoric," his "superficial and distorted tale," and pointing out that the cartoon image of the Southern Pacific as an octopus, with portraits of Leland Stanford and Charles Crocker for its eyes, long predated Norris's use of it. There would seem on the face of it to be nothing subtle in *The Octopus:* the novel is barely under way when Presley catches sight of a train, and immediately translates it into:

> the galloping monster, the terror of steel and steam, with its single eye, cyclopean, red, shooting from horizon to horizon . . . the symbol of a vast power, huge, terrible, flinging the echo of its thunder over all the reaches of the valley, leaving blood and destruction in its path; the leviathan, with tentacles of steel clutching into the soil, the soulless Force, the iron-hearted Power, the monster, the Colossus, the Octopus.

Yet *The Octopus* remains perhaps the most complex statement to date of the California condition, and a deeply ambiguous work. Nothing about the novel, on examination, is quite what it seems. Edwin Markham's "The Man with the Hoe" may have galvanized sentiment against the exploitation of labor, but it was said by its author to have been inspired, curiously, in one of the many apparent connections in California life that serve only as baffles to further inquiry, by study of a Millet painting owned by Charles Crocker, one of the Central and Southern Pacific's "Big Four," in other words a Railroad King. Frank Norris may have considered the Southern Pacific "the soulless

Force, the iron-hearted Power, the monster, the Colossus, the Octopus," but two years before he conceived the novel he was an editor of, and writing regularly for, *The Wave,* a San Francisco weekly financed by the Southern Pacific to promote Charles Crocker's new Del Monte Hotel in Monterey. *The Octopus* is not, as it might logically seem to be, a story of an agrarian society overtaken by the brute momentum of industrialization: the octopus, if there is one, turns out to be neither the railroad nor corporate ownership but indifferent nature, which is characterized, to somewhat unsettling effect, in much the same language as the railroad was earlier: "a gigantic engine, a vast cyclopean power, huge, terrible, a leviathan with a heart of steel, knowing no compunction, no forgiveness, no tolerance; crushing out the human atom standing in its way, with nirvanic calm, the agony of destruction sending never a jar. . . ."

There are, as drawn by Norris, serious ambiguities about even the climactic shootout, not the least of which are that the ranchers had never owned the land in dispute, had chosen to misread the lease agreements on the gamble that other growers would band together in such force as to render the papers useless ("Oh, rot!" one of them cries when warned to take a closer look at the leases. "Of course the railroad will sell at two-fifty. We've got the contracts"), and had taken up raising wheat on railroad land in the first place only because the railroad was there to transport the wheat. These wheat ranchers in *The Octopus* are in no sense simple farmers. They are farmers with tickers in their offices, connecting the San Joaquin by wire

with San Francisco and Chicago and New York and finally
with Liverpool, at that time the nerve center of the wheat
market. "Fluctuations in the price of the world's crop during and after the harvest," Norris wrote, "thrilled straight
to the office of Los Muertos, to that of the Quien Sabe, to
Osterman's, and to Broderson's [the ranches in the novel].
During a flurry in the Chicago wheat pits in the August of
that year, which had affected even the San Francisco market, Harran and Magnus had sat up nearly half of one
night watching the strip of white tape jerking unsteadily
from the reel."

Nor are Magnus Derrick and his son Harran and
Osterman and Broderson and Annixter even "farmers" at
all, in the conventional sense of the word: they had come
to the San Joaquin as an entrepreneurial move, after other
ventures (in mining, in politics, in whatever had presented itself) had failed or gone dry, and after, most signif-
icantly and most ambiguously, the railroad had opened
the San Joaquin to profitable cultivation by offering, for
the first time, a way to move its crops to market. The pro-
prietor of Los Muertos, Magnus Derrick, the nearest the
novel gets to a tragic hero, is nonetheless characterized by
Norris as a high-stakes gambler, a miner at heart, come to
the San Joaquin in search of the quick killing that had
eluded him in the Comstock Lode:

> It was the true California spirit that found expres-
> sion through him, the spirit of the West, unwill-
> ing to occupy itself with details, refusing to wait,
> to be patient, to achieve by legitimate plodding;

the miner's instinct of wealth acquired in a single night prevailed, in spite of all. It was in this frame of mind that Magnus and the multitude of other ranchers of whom he was a type, farmed their ranches. They had no love for their land. They were not attached to the soil. They worked their ranches as a quarter of a century before they had worked their mines. . . . To get all there was out of the land, to squeeze it dry, to exhaust it, seemed their policy. When, at last, the land worn out, would refuse to yield, they would invest their money in something else; by then, they would all have made fortunes. They did not care.

Norris's San Joaquin wheat growers, then, were of a type common enough in California: the speculators noted by Charles Nordhoff in 1874, entrepreneurs in search of the shrewd venture, men who might themselves have been running the railroad had they seen the opportunity, held the right cards, been quicker players. Confronted with the demands of the railroad (which was pressing not only to evict the ranchers but to raise freight rates) and its bought members of the Railroad Commission, the first response of the ranchers in *The Octopus* is to buy a commissioner of their own. Even in this venture not quick enough players, they buy the wrong man: Magnus Derrick's politically ambitious older son, who sells out to the railroad. That the only actual conflict in *The Octopus* turns out to be between successful and failed members of the same entrepreneurial class (members in some cases of the same families) creates a deep and troubled confusion in the novel, a dissonance its author grasped but failed to resolve. This dissonance, which had to do with the slippage between the way Californians perceived themselves and the way they were, between what they believed to be their unlimited possibilities and the limitations implicit in their own character and history, might have been Norris's great subject, but he died, at thirty-two, of peritonitis, before he could work it through. The confusions here have not been mine alone.

In the 1860s . . . William Henry Brewer [the chief assistant to Josiah Dwight Whitney in his 1860–64 geological survey of California] . . . described the southwestern San Joaquin Valley as a "plain of absolute desolation." At the turn-of-the-century, the crusading novelist Frank Norris pictured the valley as "bone dry, parched, and baked and crisped" where the "day seemed always at noon." But, a century after Brewer's report, and less than half a century after Norris's observations, it became clear that by just adding water, this vale of sterility would bloom as the nation's garden.

J ust by adding water. The above appears on the United States Bureau of Reclamation's web site, on the page prepared by the Bureau's History Program to deal with the Central Valley Project's San Luis Unit, West San Joaquin Division. We had an irrigation problem, so we *built the greatest dams the world has known,* was my equally can-do approach to the subject in "Our California Heritage." This, according to the same Bureau of Reclamation web page, is what it takes to "just add water" to the San Joaquin:

> Melting snow and runoff high in the mountains of Northern California are the first steps of a trek through the heart of the state. Once in the Sacramento–San Joaquin River Delta, water is released from storage and lifted 197 feet by the Tracy Pumping Plant. The flow is then conveyed about 70 miles south to the O'Neill Forebay via the California Aqueduct (a State Water Project, or SWP, feature) and the Federal Delta-Mendota Canal. Delta-Mendota carries water southeasterly from the Tracy Pumping Plant, eventually arriving at the O'Neill Pumping-Generating Plant. Running parallel to the Delta-Mendota Canal, the Edmund G. Brown California Aqueduct travels directly into the O'Neill Forebay. The O'Neill Dam, Pumping-Generating Plant and Forebay are all a half mile from the San Luis Dam and Reservoir. Units of the William R. Gianelli Pumping-Generating Plant (formerly known as the San Luis Pumping-Generating Plant) raises water from O'Neill Forebay into San Luis Reservoir. Releases from San Luis Reservoir are directed into the 101.3-mile-long San Luis Canal. Seventeen miles south of San Luis Reservoir, the Dos Amigos

Pumping Station lifts the water again, so the flow can continue another 85 miles across central California. Journey's end for the San Luis Canal is the Federal terminus at Kettleman City. At Kettleman City, the SWP's California Aqueduct carries on to service farms, recreational users and municipalities as far south as Los Angeles. When drought strikes California, and Delta flows cannot supply State and Federal water projects, water is released back into the O'Neill Forebay, coursing southward through the California Aqueduct. During irrigation season, water is released from the reservoir back through the pump-generator units of Gianelli to the O'Neill Forebay, generating electric power. Protecting the canal from streams crossing its path are the Los Banos and Little Panoche Detention Dams and Reservoirs. Other Unit features include the San Luis Drain, Pleasant Valley Pumping Plant, and the Coalinga Canal. The operation of the San Luis Unit is a fairly simple procedure for those brief periods when man and nature are in harmony, but both seldom have been in synchronization.

Just by adding water.
This vale of sterility would bloom as the nation's garden.
A fairly simple procedure for those brief periods when man and nature are in harmony.

The San Luis Dam, at the time it was completed in 1968, cost three billion dollars. What this taxpayer-

financed investment meant to the San Joaquin's West-
lands Water District was that several hundred growers,
most of them corporate, would have the assurance of
water, ditches, big automated Rain Birds moving all day
with the sun. These growers would also have the assurance
of "irrigation subsidies," which by 1987, according to
Gerald Haslam's *The Great Central Valley,* amounted to
twenty-seven million dollars, eleven million of which
went to the Southern Pacific Land Company. "You can't
buck the railroad" was a common phrase in my childhood,
but I never ventured into its local application.

6

HOLLISTER, the San Benito County town near which Frank Norris spent the summer of 1899 researching *The Octopus,* was named for, and built on land at that time only recently owned by, an emigrant from Ohio named William Welles Hollister. In 1852, William Welles Hollister had driven some three hundred head of cattle from Ohio to California, sold them, and returned home. In 1853, he again made the crossing, this time driving not cattle but sheep, five thousand head. This time he stayed, and over the next twenty years he and two partners, Albert and Thomas Dibblee, accumulated some two hundred thousand acres of ranch land ranging from Monterey and San Benito Counties south to Santa Barbara. William Welles Hollister was the sole owner of thirty-nine thousand acres in Santa Barbara County alone, the several ranches collectively referred to as "the Hollister ranch," which at the time of its sale in the late 1960s incorporated the twenty miles of coastline running south from Point Conception and constituted one of the last intact coastal properties of its size between the Oregon and Mexican borders.

Such extensive holdings, typically acquired on very

little equity, were not, at the time of their acquisition, entirely unusual, nor did William Welles Hollister and the Dibblee brothers even count among the largest private owners. In 1882, Richard O'Neill and James Flood together bought more than two hundred thousand acres straddling the line between Orange and San Diego Counties, a holding undivided until 1940, when the Flood heirs took the San Diego acreage and the O'Neill heirs took the Orange. Further north in Orange County, the heirs of James Irvine held the ninety-three thousand acres he had acquired in the 1870s by combining acreage originally granted to the Sepulveda and Yorba families, a property that stretched from the mountains to the sea and covered one-fifth of the county. By the time James Ben Ali Haggin and Lloyd Tevis consolidated their properties in 1890 as the Kern County Land Company, they had acquired, throughout the Southwest, almost a million and a half acres, roughly a third of them in the San Joaquin Valley. Henry Miller, another big holder, who once said that he could drive his cattle from Oregon to the Mexican border and sleep them every night on his own land, had arrived in San Francisco in 1850 with six dollars in his pocket and gone to work as a butcher. Within twenty years, he and his partner, Charles Lux, also a butcher in San Francisco, had gained control of ten to twelve million acres in California, a million and a half owned outright and grazing rights on the rest, vast tracts largely acquired through imaginative interpretation of the small print in federal legislation.

Miller, for example, made deals with cash-hungry veterans, buying up, at a discount, the land options to which they were entitled as a service benefit. He also made deft use of the federal Reclamation Act of 1850, which had granted California's "swamp and overflowed" land to the state, which in turn sold it (the "virtual gift" noted by Charles Nordhoff in 1874) for $1.15 to $1.25 an acre, an amount returned to any buyer who could demonstrate use of the land. Henry Miller was instrumental in getting large parts of California classified as swamp, in one favored telling by hooking up a team of horses to tow a rowboat over the land in question. Nor, at the time, was this even an obscure angle: *Power and Land in California,* the 1971 report prepared by the Ralph Nader Task Force and later published as *Politics of Land,* noted that two of the state surveyors responsible for classifying land as "swamp and overflowed" each left office with three hundred thousand acres.

S uch landowners tended to have not much interest in presenting themselves as the proprietors of farms or estates on the eastern, which was to say the English, model. William Henry Brewer, when he came out from Pennsylvania in 1860 to assist Josiah Dwight Whitney in the first geological survey of California, complained that the owner of eighty thousand acres between Gaviota Pass and San Luis Obispo lived "about half as well as a man would at home who owned a hundred-acre farm paid for." Almost a century later, Carey McWilliams, in *California: The Great Exception,* remarked on the almost total absence of conventional "rural" life in California, which would have been, were it a country, the world's seventh-largest agricultural producer: "The large shipper-growers 'farm by phone' from headquarters in San Francisco or Los Angeles. Many of them travel, nowadays, exclusively by plane in visiting their various 'operations.' . . . Their relationship to the land is as casual as that of the migratory workers they employ." To live as farmers would have been, for the acquisitors of these operations, a bewilderingly alien concept, since their holdings were about something else altogether: they were temporary chips in the greater game of capital formation.

This is well known, yet remains an elusive point for many Californians, particularly those with a psychic investment in one or another heightened version of the founding period. The heroine of Jack London's *The Valley of the Moon,* Saxon Brown, when hard times and union troubles come to Oakland, finds herself "dreaming of the arcadian days of her people, when they had not lived in cities nor been vexed with labor unions and employers' associations. She would remember the old people's tales of self-sufficingness, when they shot or raised their own meat, grew their own vegetables, were their own blacksmiths and carpenters, made their own shoes—yes, and spun the cloth of the clothes they wore. . . . A farmer's life must be fine, she thought. Why was it that people had to live in cities? Why had times changed?" In fact almost no one in California speaks of "farmers," in the sense the word is used in the rest of the country, and yet this persistent suggestion of constructive husbandry continues to cloud the retrospect. What amounted to the subsidized monopolization of California tends to be reinvented either as "settlement" (the settlers came, the desert bloomed) or, even more ideally, as a kind of foresighted commitment on the part of the acquisitors, a dedication to living at one with both the elemental wilderness and an improved patrician past.

"We had all shared in the glamour of immense, privately owned land," one of William Welles Hollister's seven grandchildren, Jane Hollister Wheelwright, wrote in *The Ranch Papers: A California Memoir,* the book she published in 1988, some twenty years after the sale of the Hollister ranch. "We lived in a fantastic but real world of our own discovery: square miles of impassable terrain, wild cattle threatening on the trail, single coyotes caterwauling like a pack, pumas screaming, storms felling giant oaks, washouts that marooned us for days, wildfires that lasted weeks and scorched whole mountain ranges." Her father, she tells us, "rarely wore his *chapaderos,"* and did not use his silver-inlaid saddle, "but our Mexican ranch hands knew him for what he was. They called him *'El Patrón.'*" In 1961, after the death of the father, the daughter returns alone to the ranch, the point at which there appears in her memoir the first shadow on the glamour: "No one was there to meet me—not even the ranch hands," she writes. "I had none of the honor and recognition given automatically to *El Patrón.* The ranch seemed deserted. I was being deliberately avoided. Wandering aimlessly, I found myself walking into the canyon that stretched in back of the old family home. . . . The disappointment at seeing no one quickly faded. At least the land was there to greet me."

Jane Hollister Wheelwright's sense of her entitlement seems, in *The Ranch Papers,* more layered than that of many inheritors, more complicated, even tortured. The Hollisters, she concludes, "had been given a chance to live a part of history, to experience an era virtually extinct elsewhere in California." She remains reluctant to confront the contradictions in that history. Her idea of what the land meant remains heightened, and in the familiar way. She mentions in passing that the ranch supported "a large herd of white-faced Hereford cattle," but offers no sense of a working cattle operation. She sees her father as "one of the last of the gentlemen cattlemen of the era of large family ranches in California." She tells us that she and her twin brother "had grown up in a trance, like sleepwalkers, muffled by the land's huge embrace," and accompanies a photograph of herself at twenty with an apparently meaningful quotation from Aldo Leopold's *A Sand County Almanac:* "There are two kinds of people: those who can live without wild things and those who cannot."

Yet she seems to have quite deliberately chosen, at age twenty-four, to live without wild things: she married a psychiatrist, Joseph Wheelwright, was herself analyzed by Carl Jung, became a lay analyst, gave birth to a daughter in China and a son in London, and returned to California with her husband to found, in 1943 in San Francisco, the world's first Jungian training center. The description she gives of her 1961 return to the ranch is suggestive. All such returns, she tells us, involved a learned process of "reaching into the mood of the place," of shedding "city demands." She had come to understand the necessity of cultivating "calming" through "the monotony of walk-ing," of encouraging the accelerated onset of what others might call by other names but she called "the big let-down": "Our coast requires a descent always. For those new to the place the letdown is more often experienced as an unpleasant locked-in feeling, an immobilizing depression."

What we seem to have here, then, is a story of an acquisitive grandfather, a father who retreated into the huge holding that allowed him to play *El Patrón* (even the daughter who reveres him mentions, in the guise of a virtue, "his power of passivity"), and a daughter, Jane Hollister, who ran guiltily for daylight. It was nonetheless Jane Hollister Wheelwright, not her brothers or cousins, who inherited from the father in 1961 the power to vote more than half the shares in the ranches. "My father must have known that I was as stubborn as he and would try to tackle the problems; and as the only woman I would be outside male competition," she wrote in *The Ranch Papers*. "But the outrage it caused only compounded the existing situation, and so the struggle began amongst the seven of us." That the nature of this struggle is not described in *The Ranch Papers* is a telling lacuna. It would appear to have focused, since the need to sell was a given, on the terms of the sale: to whom, for how much, in return for what contingent agreements. One senses that the daugh-ter may have favored, probably more than her brothers and cousins did, the ultimate buyer: a Los Angeles devel-oper, described in *The Ranch Papers,* again ideally, as "an enterprising but environment-minded Los Angeles man," whose plan was to rezone the property into hundred-acre parcels and present the whole as an exclusive planned retreat.

In California as elsewhere, a buyer with a plan for this kind of low-density development signifies something quite specific: this is a buyer who means to pay less for the land than one with a plan for more intensive development. During the same years when the Hollisters were falling out over this issue, James Irvine's great-granddaughter, Joan Irvine Smith, someone else who had "shared in the glamour of immensely, privately owned land," was fighting the same kind of family fight, but from a different angle: it was Joan Irvine who successfully insisted, against the opposition of some in her own family, that the eighty-eight thousand acres that remained of the Irvine ranch in Orange County be intensively developed. Whether Jane Hollister's decision to divide her grandfather's ranch into hundred-acre parcels was in the end more intrinsically tuned to the spirit of the place than Joan Irvine's quite different decision remains an unresolved question. I recall in the early seventies seeing advertising for what came to be called "Hollister Ranch," emphasizing how very few select achievers could hope to live there. As it happens my father had been at Berkeley with one of the Hollisters, someone of an age to have been one of Jane Hollister's brothers or cousins; I do not remember his name and my father is dead. I remember this at all only because, every time we drove south and again at the time the ranch was sold, my father mentioned that the effort to keep their holding intact had left the Hollisters unable to afford, in the early 1930s, during the Depression, to let one of their children finish Berkeley. This was offered as a lesson, I am unsure to what point.

The lesson Jane Hollister Wheelwright took from the sale of her family's ranch, proceeding as she did from within what amounts to a fable of confusion, concerned what she called the "debatable" questions: "whether land can belong to anyone, or whether one belongs to the land." She concluded, unsurprisingly, that land belonged to no one. Yet it did: at the time the Hollister ranch was sold, in the late 1960s, according to a Ralph Nader Study Group report on land use in California, roughly two and a half million acres of California still belonged to the Southern Pacific. Almost half a million acres belonged to the Shasta Forest Company. A third of a million acres belonged to Tenneco, another third of a million each to the Tejon Ranch Company, Standard Oil, and Boise Cascade. Two hundred seventy-eight thousand acres belonged to Georgia Pacific. Two hundred and fifty thousand belonged to Pacific Gas & Electric. Two hundred thousand belonged to Occidental Petroleum, 192,000 to Sunkist, 171,062 to Pacific Lumber, 155,000 to Fibreboard Incorporated, and 152,000 to the Newhall Land and Farming Company. Another 1,350,045 acres belonged to, among them, American Forest Products, Times Mirror, the Penn Central, Hammond Lumber, Kaiser Industries, the Masonite Corporation, J. G. Boswell, International Paper, Diamond International Corporation, Vail, Miller & Lux, and the

Irvine Ranch Company. Some of these were California companies; some were not. All played a role in determining which of California's possibilities would be realized and which limited. Most were diversified, no more interested in what grew or grazed on their land than Jane Hollister had been, to another point, in what grew or grazed on hers, but quicker players, all of them, than the Hollisters had proved to be.

J ane Hollister's mother, Lottie Steffens Hollister, was the sister of Lincoln Steffens, who wrote *The Shame of the Cities* and later said of the Soviet Union that he had seen the future and it worked. Lincoln Steffens was Jane Hollister's "Uncle Steffie," and she his "Lady Jane." The Steffens children had grown up in a house in Sacramento a few blocks from the house in which, in 1908, my father was born. The Steffens house later became the Governor's Mansion, in which both Jerry Brown and his sister Kathleen lived during the years their father, Edmund G. ("Pat") Brown, was the thirty-second governor of California. Jerry Brown was himself the thirty-fourth governor of California. Kathleen Brown, in 1994, tried and failed to become the thirty-seventh. I went to Berkeley with their sister Barbara. There are many connections in California life, and yet, like Charles Crocker's Millet as the source for Edwin Markham's "The Man with the Hoe," not much connects: my mother's father, who lived in Sacramento but grew up on the Georgetown Divide in El Dorado County, remained convinced to his death that

Edwin Markham, who had been superintendent of schools in El Dorado County from 1882 until 1886, did not himself write "The Man with the Hoe," but was given the poem by, in my grandfather's words, "an emigrant wayfarer from whom Markham purchased it for a small amount of money, and thereby helped the traveler along his way." My grandfather seemed to have in his memory bank a fairly complete dossier on Edwin Markham (the names of his three wives, the dates of his and their arrivals in California, even the houses in which they had lived), and could be quite insistent about what he believed to be the true provenance of "The Man with the Hoe," but his attitude toward the alleged appropriation was sufficiently opaque to encourage me, as a child, to ask my mother if my grandfather had in fact been the emigrant wayfarer. "He wasn't an emigrant," my mother said, settling at least that question.

Jane Hollister Wheelwright, who was herself born in Sacramento, saw as a kind of death the intrusion onto the Hollister ranch of two Chevron pipelines ("I can only believe that their appearance on the ranch means just one thing: another expression of man's historical arrogance and hatred of nature") but, still operating within the fable of an ideal personal past, was untroubled, even comforted, by the presence of the Southern Pacific, which her grandfather had actively supported and to which he had given a sixty-foot right-of-way along the coast. On her farewell rides through the ranch she observed the daily appearance of *The Daylight,* the Southern Pacific's principal passenger train to Los Angeles, and noted that it "seemed to belong there, and did not jar the feeling of the coast in the slightest. The noises it made recalled my childhood when we had no other way of telling time, and the sound of a whistle in the distance meant we were hopelessly late for lunch."

The eighth governor of California, Leland Stanford, was at the time of his election the president of the Central Pacific and later the president of the Southern Pacific. Hiram Johnson, the twenty-third governor of California, was elected as a reform candidate pledged to break the power of the Southern Pacific. Hiram Johnson's father, Grove Johnson, had fled upstate New York under indictment for forgery in 1863, settled in Sacramento, become clerk of the county Swamp Land Board, been implicated in two vote-rigging scandals, and been elected, in 1877, to the California State Assembly. "The interests of the railroad and Sacramento are identical, and should always remain so," the elder Johnson declared during this campaign. "They should labor together like man and wife, only to be divorced by death."

When Hiram Johnson went to Berkeley in 1884 he lived in the Chi Phi house, as did, forty-five years later, my father and my uncle and the Hollister who had to drop out of school. When I went to Berkeley some years later I lived, as did Barbara Brown, at the Tri Delt house. Her father, not yet governor of California but its attorney general, spoke at our annual father-daughter dinners. When my brother went to Berkeley five years after I did he lived at the Phi Gamma Delta, or Fiji, house, as had, sixty-some years before, Frank Norris, who remained famous in the house for having initiated its annual celebratory "Pig Dinner." This was a California, into the nineteen-fifties, so hermetic, so isolated by geography and by history and also by inclination, that when I first read *The Octopus,* at age twelve or thirteen, in Sacramento, I did not construe it to have a personal relevance, since the events described took place not in the Sacramento Valley but somewhere else, the San Joaquin.

Not much about California, on its own preferred terms, has encouraged its children to see themselves as connected to one another. The separation, of north from south—and even more acutely of west from east, of the urban coast from the agricultural valleys and of both the coast and the valleys from the mountain and desert regions to their east—was profound, fueled by the rancor of water wars and by less tangible but even more rancorous differences in attitude and culture. My mother made the trip from Sacramento to Los Angeles in 1932, to see the Olympics, and did not find reason to make it again for thirty years. In the north we had San Francisco, with its Beaux Arts buildings and eucalyptus, its yearnings backward and westward, its resolutely anecdotal "color"; a place as remote and mannered as the melancholy colonial capitals of Latin America, and as isolated. When I was at Berkeley and had gone home to Sacramento for a weekend I would sometimes take the Southern Pacific's transcontinental *City of San Francisco* back down, not the most convenient train (for one thing it was always late) but one that suggested, carrying as it did the glamour of having come across the mountains from the rest of America, that our isolation might not be an indefinite sentence.

I see now that the life I was raised to admire was entirely the product of this isolation, infinitely romantic, but in a kind of vacuum, its only antecedent aesthetic, and the aesthetic only the determined "Bohemianism" of nineteenth-century San Francisco. The clothes chosen for me as a child had a strong element of the Pre-Raphaelite, muted greens and ivories, dusty rose, what seems in retrospect an eccentric amount of black. I still have the black mantilla I was given to wear over my shoulders when I started to go to dances, not the kind of handkerchief triangle Catholic woman used to keep in their pockets and glove compartments but several yards of heavy black lace. It had been my great-grandmother's, I have no idea why, since this particular great-grandmother was from Oregon, with no reason to have bought into a romance-of-the-ranchos scenario. We lived in dark houses and favored, a preference so definite that it passed as a test of character, copper and brass that had darkened and greened. We also let our silver darken, which was said to "bring out the pattern." To this day I am put off by highly polished silver: it looks "new." This predilection for the "old" extended into all areas of domestic life: dried flowers were seen to have a more subtle charm than fresh, prints should be faded, rugs worn, wallpaper streaked by the sun. Our highest moment in this area was the acquisition, in 1951, of a house in Sacramento in which the curtains on the stairs had not been changed since 1907. These curtains, which were of unlined (and faded, naturally) gold silk organza, hung almost two stories, billowed iridescent with every breath of air, and, if touched, crumbled.

Stressing as it did an extreme if ungrounded individualism, this was not an ambiance that tended toward a view of life as defined or limited or controlled, or even in any way affected, by the social and economic structures of the larger world. To be a Californian was to see oneself, if one believed the lessons the place seemed most immediately to offer, as affected only by "nature," which in turn was seen to exist simultaneously as a source of inspiration or renewal ("Born again!" John Muir noted in the journal of his first trip into Yosemite) and as the ultimate brute reckoning, the force that by guaranteeing destruction gave the place its perilous beauty. Much of the California landscape has tended to present itself as metaphor, even as litany: the redwoods *(for a thousand years in thy sight are but as yesterday)*, the Mojave *(in the midst of life we are in death)*, the coast at Big Sur, Mono Lake, the great vistas of the Sierra, especially those of the Yosemite Valley, which, Kevin Starr has pointed out, "offered Californians an objective correlative for their ideal sense of themselves: a people animated by heroic imperatives." Thomas Starr King saw Yosemite in 1860 and went back to the First Unitarian Church of San Francisco determined to inspire "Yosemites in the soul." Albert Bierstadt saw Yosemite in 1863 and came back to do the grandiose landscapes that made him for a dozen years the most popularly acclaimed painter in America. "Some of Mr. Bierstadt's mountains swim in a lustrous, pearly mist," Mark Twain observed with some acerbity, "which is so enchantingly beautiful that I am sorry the Creator hadn't made it instead of him, so that it would always remain there."

Lessons could be found even in less obviously histrionic features: climbing Mt. Tamalpais in Marin County at sunrise was seen, in my grandmother's generation, as a convenient transformative experience, as was any contemplation of the opening to the Pacific that John C. Frémont, when he mapped the area in 1846, had named "Chrysopylae," or Golden Gate, "on the same principle that the harbor of Byzantium (Constantinople afterwards) was called Chrysoceras (golden horn)." Josiah Royce, in his 1879 essay "Meditation Before the Gate," reflected on the view of the Gate from Berkeley and pledged himself to pursue his philosophical inquiries "independently, because I am a Californian, as little bound to follow mere tradition as I am liable to find an audience by preaching in this wilderness; reverently, because I am thinking and writing face to face with a mighty and lovely Nature, by the side of whose greatness I am but as a worm."

This is interesting, a quite naked expression of what has been the California conundrum. Scaled against Yosemite, or against the view through the Gate of the Pacific trembling on its tectonic plates, the slightest shift of which could and with some regularity did destroy the works of man in a millisecond, all human beings were of course but as worms, their "heroic imperatives" finally futile, their philosophical inquiries vain. The population of California has increased in my lifetime from six million to close to thirty-five million people, yet the three phrases that come first to mind when I try to define California to myself refer exclusively to its topography, a landscape quite empty of people. The first of these phrases comes from the language of broadcast weather reports, the second from John Muir. The third, and most persistent, comes from Robinson Jeffers. *Point Conception to the Mexican border. The Range of Light. Beautiful country burn again, / Point Pinos down to the Sur Rivers.*

This is the point in the California experience when discussion stops, and many voices fade. Broadcast weather reports could be seen as nominally neutral on the question of whether human beings have any rightful place in California, but John Muir and Robinson Jeffers could not. Muir traded the Calvinism of his Scottish childhood for an equally Calvinist wilderness, a landscape in which he could tolerate only Indians, because Indians "walk softly and hurt the landscape hardly more than the birds and squirrels, and their brush and bark huts last hardly longer than those of woodrats, while their more enduring monuments, excepting those wrought on the forests by the fires they made to improve their hunting grounds, vanish in a few centuries." Jeffers tolerated no one at all, taking this aversion to the point at which he came to favor war, which alone, as he saw it, could return the world to its "emptiness," to "the bone, the colorless white bone, the excellence." "Be in nothing so moderate as in love of man," he advised his twin sons, and referred to mankind as a "botched experiment that has run wild and ought to be stopped." He was accused of "proto-fascism." He called himself an "Inhumanist." (As in, from a posting on the Jeffers Studies web site, "I'm interested in the relationship between Inhumanism and Deep Ecology and would welcome any thoughts or comments.") He seemed to many an easy target: his poetry could be pretentious, his postures ugly. Read in situ, however, Jeffers makes fatally seductive sense: *Burn as before with bitter wonders, land and ocean and the Carmel water.* And: *When the cities lie at the monster's feet there are left the mountains.*

I am thinking and writing face to face with a mighty and lovely Nature, Josiah Royce wrote, *by the side of whose greatness I am but as a worm.* Royce in fact seems to have maintained an exhausting but finally vain alert against the undertow of this localized nihilism. His 1886 *California: A Study of American Character* bore on its title page these peculiar but premonitory lines, spoken by Mephistopheles in the Prologue to *Faust: On suns and worlds I can shed little light / I see but humans, and their piteous plight.* At sixty, in despair at the prospect of World War One and a few months short of what would be a fatal stroke, he encountered in Harvard Yard one of his students, Horace Kallen, who, according to Robert V. Hine's *Josiah Royce: From Grass Valley to Harvard,* reported of Royce that "When I greeted him, his round blue eyes looked staring, and without recognition. And then he said in a voice somehow thinner . . . 'You are on the side of humanity, aren't you?' " A few months before, describing himself as "socially ineffective as regards genuine 'team play,' ignorant of politics, an ineffective member of committees, and a poor helper of concrete social enterprises," as well as "a good deal of a non-conformist, and disposed to a certain rebellion," Royce had acknowledged that the idea of community to which he had devoted his career remained in some way alien to him: "When I review this whole process, I strongly feel that my deepest motives and problems have centered about the Idea of the Community, although this idea has only come gradually to my clear consciousness. This is what I was intensely feeling, in the days when my sisters and I looked across the Sacramento Valley, and wondered about the great world beyond our mountains. . . . So much of the spirit that opposes the community I have and have always had in me, simply, deeply, elementally."

So much of the spirit that opposes the community: of course he had it in him, considering what he was: ". . . *because I am a Californian,*" he himself had written, "*as little bound to follow mere tradition. . . .*" In 1970 I spent a month in the South, in Louisiana and Alabama and Mississippi, under the misapprehension that an understanding of the differences between the West and the South, which had given California a good deal of its original settlement, would improve my understanding of California. Royce had fretted over the same question: "Very early . . . this relatively peaceful mingling of Americans from North and South had already deeply affected the tone of California life," he noted in *California: A Study of American Character.* "The type of the Northern man who has assumed Southern fashions, and not always the best Southern fashions at that, has often been observed in California life. . . . He often followed the Southerner, and was frequently, in time, partly assimilated by the Southern civilization." One difference between the West and the South, I came to realize in 1970, was this: in the South they remained convinced that they had bloodied their land with history. In California we did not believe that history could bloody the land, or even touch it.

7

THOMAS KINKADE was born in the late 1950s and raised in Placerville, El Dorado County, where his mother supported him and his siblings by working as a notary public, piecework, five dollars a document. The father had left. The family lived much of the time in a trailer. By the early 1990s "Thomas Kinkade" was a phenomenon, a brand on his own, a merchandiser who could touch a snow globe or a stoneware mug or a night-light or a La-Z-Boy chair with the magic of his name and turn it to money, a painter so successful that by the end of the decade there would be throughout the United States 248 Thomas Kinkade "signature galleries," seventy-eight of them in California alone, most of those in malls or tourist areas, four for example in Monterey and another four in Carmel, two exits down Highway 1. Since very few of Thomas Kinkade's original oil paintings were by that time available, and since those that were had risen in price from about $15,000 in the early 1990s to more than $300,000 by 1997, the pictures sold in these 248 "signature galleries" were canvas-backed reproductions, which themselves sold for $900 to $15,000 and were produced by the 450 employees who labored in the hundred-thousand-square-foot Morgan Hill headquarters of Media Arts Group Incorporated ("MDA" on the New York Stock Exchange), the business of which was Thomas Kinkade.

The passion with which buyers approached these Kinkade images was hard to define. The manager of one California gallery that handled them told me that it was not unusual to sell six or seven at a clip, to buyers who already owned ten or twenty, and that the buyers with whom he dealt brought to the viewing of the images "a sizeable emotional weight." A Kinkade painting was typically rendered in slightly surreal pastels. It typically featured a cottage or a house of such insistent coziness as to seem actually sinister, suggestive of a trap designed to attract Hansel and Gretel. Every window was lit, to lurid effect, as if the interior of the structure might be on fire. The cottages had thatched roofs, and resembled gingerbread houses. The houses were Victorian, and resembled idealized bed-and-breakfasts, at least two of which in Placerville, the Chichester-McKee House and the Combellack-Blair House, claimed to have been the models for Kinkade "Christmas" paintings. "There's a lot of beauty here that I present in a way that's whimsical and charming," Kinkade allowed to the Placerville *Mountain Democrat*. He branded himself the "Painter of Light," and the postcards Media Arts provided to his galleries each for a while bore this legend: "Thomas Kinkade is recognized as the foremost living painter of light. His masterful use of soft edges and luminous colors give his highly detailed oil paintings a glow all their own. This extraordinary 'Kinkade Glow' has created an overwhelming demand for Thomas Kinkade paintings and lithographs worldwide."

This "Kinkade Glow" could be seen as derived in spirit from the "lustrous, pearly mist" that Mark Twain had derided in the Bierstadt paintings, and, the level of execution to one side, there are certain unsettling similarities between the two painters. "After completing my recent plein air study of Yosemite Valley, the mountains' majesty refused to leave me," Kinkade wrote in June 2000 on his web site. "When my family wandered through the national park visitor center, I discovered a key to my fantasy—a recreation of a Miwok Indian Village. When I returned to my studio, I began work on *The Mountains Declare His Glory,* a poetic expression of what I felt at that transforming moment of inspiration. As a final touch, I even added a Miwok Indian Camp along the river as an affirmation that man has his place, even in a setting touched by God's glory."

Affirming that man has his place in the Sierra Nevada by reproducing the Yosemite National Park Visitor Center's recreation of a Miwok Indian Village is identifiable as a doubtful enterprise on many levels (not the least of which being that the Yosemite Miwok were forcibly run onto a reservation near Fresno during the Gold Rush, and allowed to return to Yosemite only in 1855), but is Thomas Kinkade's Sierra in fact any more sentimentalized than that of Albert Bierstadt? Were not the divinely illuminated passes of Bierstadt's Sierra meant to confirm the successful completion of our manifest destiny? Was it by chance that Collis P. Huntington commissioned Bierstadt to undertake a painting celebrating the domination of Donner Pass by the Central Pacific Railroad? Was not Bierstadt's triumphalist *Donner Lake from the Summit* a willful revision to this point of the locale that most clearly embodied the moral ambiguity of the California settlement? This was the lesson drawn from the pass in question by one of the surviving children of the Donner Party, Virginia Reed, who wrote to her cousin: "Oh, Mary, I have not wrote you half of the trouble we've had, but I have wrote you enough to let you know what trouble is. But thank God, we are the only family that did not eat human flesh. We have left everything, but I don't care for that. We have got through with our lives. Don't let this letter dishearten anybody. Remember, never take no cutoffs and hurry along as fast as you can."

Remember, never take no cutoffs and hurry along as fast as you can.

Did the preferred version of our history reflect the artless horror and constricted moral horizon of Virginia Reed's firsthand account?

Or had it come more closely to resemble the inspirational improvement that was Bierstadt's *Donner Lake from the Summit*?

The confusions embedded in the crossing story can be seen in unintended relief in Jack London's *The Valley of the Moon*, the 1913 novel that has at its center the young woman Saxon Brown. At the time we meet Saxon she is orphaned, boarding with her hard-pressed socialist brother and his bad-tempered wife, and spending six hard days a week as a piecework ironer in an Oakland laundry. On their Saturday night off, Saxon and a friend from the laundry splurge on tickets to a Bricklayers' picnic, where Saxon meets a similarly orphaned teamster, Billy Roberts, to whom she confides that she was named for "the first English, and you know the Americans came from the English. We're Saxons, you an' me, an' Mary, an' Bert, and all the Americans that are real Americans, you know, and not Dagoes and Japs and such." If this seems a thin reed on which to hang one's identity, it would not have seemed so to London, who, Kevin Starr noted in *Americans and the California Dream,* once protested an arrest for vagrancy by arguing to the court "that no old American whose ancestors had fought in the American Revolution should be treated this way." The moment in which the judge nonetheless sentenced him to thirty days is described by Starr as "one of the most traumatic" in London's life.

Assured by Billy Roberts that he too is a "real" American, that his mother's family "crossed to Maine hundreds of years ago," Saxon asks where his father was from. This extraordinary exchange ensues:

"Don't know." Billy shrugged his shoulders. "He didn't know himself. Nobody ever knew, though he was American, all right, all right."

"His name's regular old American," Saxon suggested. "There's a big English general right now whose name is Roberts. I've read it in the papers."

"But Roberts wasn't my father's name. He never knew what his name was. Roberts was the name of a gold-miner who adopted him. You see, it was this way. When they was Indian-fightin' up there with the Modoc Indians, a lot of miners an' settlers took a hand. Roberts was captain of one outfit, and once, after a fight, they took a lot of prisoners—squaws, an' kids an' babies. An' one of the kids was my father. They figured he was about five years old. He didn't know nothin' but Indian."

Saxon clapped her hands, and her eyes sparkled: "He'd been captured on an Indian raid!"

"That's the way they figured it," Billy nodded. "They recollected a wagon-train of Oregon settlers that'd been killed by the Modocs four years before. Roberts adopted him, and that's why I don't know his real name. But you can bank on it, he crossed the plains just the same."

"So did my father," Saxon said proudly.

"An' my mother, too," Billy added, pride touching his own voice. "Anyway, she came pretty close to crossin' the plains, because she was born in a wagon on the River Platte on the way out."

"My mother, too," said Saxon. "She was eight years old, an' she walked most of the way after the oxen began to give out."

Billy thrust out his hand.

"Put her there, kid," he said. "We're just like old friends, what with the same kind of folks behind us."

With shining eyes, Saxon extended her hand to his, and gravely they shook.

"Isn't it wonderful?" she murmured. "We're both old American stock."

To assume that London was employing irony here, that his intention was to underline the distance between Saxon and Billy's actual situation and their illusions of superior lineage, would be to misread *The Valley of the Moon*. "Times have changed," Saxon complains to Billy. "We crossed the plains and opened up this country, and now we're losing even the chance to work for a living in it." This strikes a chord in Billy, which resonates again when the two happen into a prosperous Portuguese settlement: "It looks like the free-born American ain't got no room left in his own land," Billy says to Saxon. A further thought from Billy: "It was our folks who made this country. Fought for it, opened it up, did everything—"

This truculence on the question of immigration was by no means an unfamiliar note in California, which by the time London wrote already had a tenacious history of vigilance committees and exclusionary legislation. "The fearful blindness of the early behavior of the Americans in California towards foreigners is something almost unintelligible," Josiah Royce wrote in 1886 of the violence and lynchings to which "foreigners"—mainly Sonorans but also Chinese and native Digger Indians—had been subjected in the gold fields. Sixty-some years after Royce, Carey McWilliams, in *California: The Great Exception,* characterized the pervasive local hostility toward Asians as "a social and psychic necessity of the situation," the "negative device" by which a state made up of newly arrived strangers had been able to achieve the illusion of a cohesive community joined against the menace of the foreign-born.

Such hostility was by no means unknown in more settled parts of the country, but rarely was it so intricately codified by law. The Foreign Miners' License Tax of 1850 had exacted a monthly fee of any non-citizen who wanted to work a claim. In 1854, an existing law prohibiting Negroes and Indians from testifying in court had been extended to also prohibit testimony by Chinese. The state legislature had barred "Mongolians, Indians, and Negroes" from public schools in 1860; had barred Chinese from employment in corporations or on public works projects in 1879; and had amended an existing miscegenation law to include Chinese in 1906. The state Alien Land Acts of 1913 and 1920 would for more than thirty years effectively prohibit land ownership in California to both Asians and their American-born children.

It was in this spirit that the two "real" Americans, Saxon and Billy, set out in search of government land, the 160 free acres which were, as they saw it, their due. This conviction of entitlement was another familiar California note, and a particularly complicated one, since the idea of depending on the government of course ran counter to the preferred self-image of most Californians. Yet such dependence was, even then, almost total. It had been, as we have seen, federal money, spent on behalf of a broad spectrum of business interests, that built the railroad and opened the state to the rest of the world. It had been and would be, as we have seen, federal money, again spent on behalf of a large spectrum of business interests, that created what was no longer locally even called agribusiness, just "ag." The rationalization that resolves this contradiction is, in *The Valley of the Moon,* fairly primitive: the government owes Saxon and Billy free land, Billy reasons, "for what our fathers an' mothers done. I tell you, Saxon, when a woman walks across the plains like your mother done, an' a man an' wife gets massacred by the Indians like my grandfather an' mother done, the government does owe them something."

The land on which Saxon and Billy finally settle is the actual Valley of the Moon, in Sonoma County, and their discovery of it prefigures many of the doubtful sentiments that would later surface in the paintings of Thomas Kinkade. They arrive in the valley just as "sunset fires, refracted from the cloud-driftage of the autumn sky" turn the landscape "crimson." They see a stream, "singing" to them. They see "fairy circles" of redwoods. They see, at a distance, a man and a woman, "side by side, the delicate hand of the woman curled in the hand of the man, which looked as if made to confer benedictions." This magical bonding continues, again as if touched by the Kinkade Glow:

Perhaps the picture made by Saxon and Billy was equally arresting and beautiful, as they drove down through the golden end of day. The two couples had eyes only for each other. The little

woman beamed joyously. The man's face glowed
into the benediction that had trembled there. To
Saxon, like the field up the mountain, like the
mountain itself, it seemed that she had always
known this adorable pair. She knew that she loved
them.

Only later does Saxon discover what the reader (by
this point almost four hundred pages into *The Valley of the
Moon*) may well have suspected early on: "this adorable
pair" are in fact "old stock that had crossed the Plains,"
keepers perhaps of their own iconic potato masher, in any
event kindred souls who "knew all about the fight at Little
Meadow, and the tale of the massacre of the emigrant train
of which Billy's father had been the sole survivor." Their
rightful place in the California fable validated, Saxon and
Billy settle in, determined to redeem the birthright of the
"old stock" through the practice of scientific agronomy,
which London himself imagined that he and his second
wife, the woman he called his "Mate-Woman," Charmian
Kittredge, were perfecting on their own Sonoma ranch.
London's letters from this period speak of "making the
dead soil live again," of leaving the land "better for my
having been," of unremitting industry, transcendent husbandry. "No picayune methods for me," he wrote. "When
I go in silence, I want to know that I left behind me a plot
of land which, after the pitiful failures of others, I have
made productive. . . . Can't you see? Oh, try to see!—In
the solution of great economic problems of the present
age, I see a return to the soil."

This was another confusion. His crops failed. His Wolf House, built to last a thousand years, burned to the ground before he and the Mate-Woman (or, as he alternately called Charmian, the Wolf-Mate) could move in. His health was gone. He battled depression. He battled alcoholism. At one point in 1913, the year Wolf House was completed and burned, he had only three dollars and forty-six cents left in the bank. In the end only the Mate-Woman kept the faith: "I am crazy for everyone to know about Jack's big experiment up here," Charmian Kittredge London wrote to a friend, Tom Wilkinson, on December 15, 1916. "So few persons think of it at all in connection with him—they slobber about his this and his that and his the other, and say nothing about his tremendous experiment—practical experiment—up here on Sonoma Mountain." Just three weeks before this letter was written, Jack London had died, at forty, of uremic poisoning and one final, fatal, dose of the morphine prescribed to calm his renal colic. In the last novel he was to write, *The Little Lady of the Big House,* he had allowed his protagonist and author-surrogate to ask these questions, a flash of the endemic empty in a work that is otherwise a fantasy of worldly and social success: "Why? What for? What's it worth? What's it all about?"

8

THE Bohemian Club of San Francisco was founded, in 1872, by members of the city's working press, who saw it both as a declaration of unconventional or "artistic" interests and as a place to get a beer and a sandwich after the bulldog closed. Frank Norris was a member, as was Henry George, who had not yet published *Progress and Poverty.* There were poets: Joaquin Miller, George Sterling. There were writers: Samuel Clemens, Bret Harte, Ambrose Bierce, Jack London, who only a few months before his death managed to spend a week at Bohemian Grove, the club's encampment in the redwoods north of San Francisco. John Muir belonged to the Bohemian Club, and so did Joseph LeConte. For a few years the members appear to have remained resolute in their determination not to admit the merely rich (they had refused membership to William C. Ralston, the president of the Bank of California), but their over-ambitious spending, both on the club in town and on its periodic encampments, quite soon overwhelmed this intention. According to a memoir of the period written by Edward Bosqui, San Francisco's most prominent publisher during the late nineteenth century and a charter member of the Bohemian

Club, it was at this point decided to "invite an element to join the club which the majority of the members held in contempt, namely men who had money as well as brains, but who were not, strictly speaking, Bohemians."

By 1927, a year after George Sterling committed suicide during a club dinner for H. L. Mencken by going upstairs to bed and swallowing cyanide (he had been depressed, he had been drinking, Frank Norris's brother had replaced him as toastmaster for the Mencken dinner), the Bohemian Club was banning from its annual art exhibit any entry deemed by the club "in radical and unreasonable departure from laws of art." By 1974, when G. William Domhoff, then a professor of sociology at the University of California at Santa Cruz, wrote *The Bohemian Grove and Other Retreats: A Study in Ruling-Class Cohesiveness,* one in five resident members and one in three nonresident members of the Bohemian Club was listed in *Standard & Poor's Register of Corporations, Executives, and Directors.* Among those attending the summer encampment at Bohemian Grove in 1970, the year for which Domhoff obtained a list, "at least one officer or director from forty of the fifty largest industrial corporations in America was present. . . . Similarly, we found that officers and directors from twenty of the top twenty-five commercial banks (including all of the fifteen largest) were on our lists. Men from twelve of the first twenty-five life-insurance companies were in attendance (eight of these twelve were from the top ten)."

The summer encampment, then, had evolved into a special kind of enchanted circle, one in which these captains of American finance and industry could entertain, in what was to most of them an attractively remote setting, the temporary management of that political structure on which their own fortunes ultimately depended. When Dwight Eisenhower visited the Grove in 1950, eleven years before he made public his concern about the military-industrial complex, he traveled on a special train arranged by the president of the Santa Fe Railroad. Domhoff noted that both Henry Kissinger and Melvin Laird, then secretary of defense, were present at the 1970 encampment, as were David M. Kennedy, then secretary of the treasury, and Admiral Thomas H. Moorer, chairman of the Joint Chiefs of Staff. John Erlichman, as the guest of Leonard Firestone, represented the White House. Walter J. Hickel, at the time secretary of the interior, was the guest of Fred L. Hartley, the president of Union Oil.

The rituals of the summer encampment were fixed. There were, every day at twelve-thirty, "Lakeside Talks," informal speeches and briefings, off the record. Kissinger, Laird, and William P. Rogers, then secretary of state, gave Lakeside Talks in 1970; Colin Powell and the chairman of Dow Chemical were scheduled for 1999. Local color was measured: the fight songs sung remained those of the traditional California schools, Berkeley (or, in this venue, "Cal") and Stanford, yet it was a rule of the Bohemian Club that no Californian, unless he was a member, could be asked as a guest during the two-week midsummer encampment. (As opposed to the May "Spring Jinks" weekend, to which California non-members could be invited.) The list for the 1985 encampment, the most recent complete roster I have seen, shows the members and their "camps," the hundred-some self-selected groupings situated back through the hills and canyons and off the road to the Russian River. Each camp has a name. for example Stowaway, or Pink Onion, or Silverado Squatters, or Lost Angels.

For the 1985 encampment, Caspar Weinberger was due at Isle of Aves, James Baker III at Woof. "George H. W. Bush" appeared on the list for Hillbillies (his son, George W. Bush, seems not to have been present in 1985, but he was on the list, along with his father and Newt Gingrich, for 1999), as did, among others, Frank Borman, William F. Buckley, Jr., and his son Christopher, Walter Cronkite, A. W. Clausen of the Bank of America and the World Bank, and Frank A. Sprole of Bristol-Myers. George Shultz was on the list for Mandalay, along with William French Smith, Thomas Watson, Jr., Nicholas Brady, Leonard K. Firestone, Peter Flanigan, Gerald Ford, Najeeb Halaby, Philip M. Hawley, J. K. Horton, Edgar F. Kaiser, Jr., Henry Kissinger, John McCone, and two of the Bechtels. This virtual personification of Eisenhower's military-industrial complex notwithstanding, the Spirit of Bohemia, or California, could still be seen, in the traditional tableaux performed at every Grove encampment, to triumph over Mammon, God of Gold, and all his gnomes and promises and bags of treasure:

SPIRIT: *Nay, Mammon. For one thing it cannot buy.*
MAMMON: *What cannot it buy?*
SPIRIT: *A happy heart!*

seemed temperamentally unable to consider an "average Californian" who would not, in the end, see that his own best interests lay in cooperation, in the amelioration of differences, in a certain willingness to forego the immediate windfall for the larger or even his own long-term good. This was the same "average Californian" who, by the year Royce wrote, 1886, had already sold half the state to the Southern Pacific and was in the process of mortgaging the rest to the federal government. For most of the next hundred years, kept aloft first by oil and then by World War Two and finally by the Cold War and the largesse of the owners and managers who would arrive in Gulfstreams for the annual encampment at Bohemian Grove, that average Californian had seen his "easiest failing" yield only blue skies.

The transformation of the Bohemian Club from a lively if frivolous gathering of local free spirits to a nexus of the nation's corporate and political interests in many ways mirrored a larger transformation, that of California itself from what it had been, or from what its citizens preferred to believe that it had been, to what it is now, an entirely dependent colony of the invisible empire in which those corporate and political interests are joined. In 1868, four years before he helped to found the Bohemian Club, Henry George, twenty-nine years old and previously unpublished, wrote a piece in the *Overland Monthly* in which he tried to locate "the peculiar charm of California, which all who have lived here long enough feel." He concluded that California's charm resided in the character of its people: ". . . there has been a feeling of personal independence and equality, a general hopefulness and self-reliance, and a certain large-heartedness and open-handedness which were born of the comparative evenness with which property was distributed, the high standard of wages and of comfort, and the latent feeling of everyone that he might 'make a strike.'" This piece, "What the Railroad Will Bring Us," was intended, of course, as an antidote to the enthusiasm then general about the windfall to be realized by giving the state to the Southern Pacific:

Let us see clearly whither we are tending. Increase in population and in wealth past a certain point means simply an approximation to the condition of older countries—the eastern states and Europe. . . . The truth is, that the completion of the railroad and the consequent great increase of business and population, will not be a benefit to all of us, but only to a portion. . . . This crowding of people into immense cities, this aggregation of wealth into large lumps, this marshalling of men into big gangs under the control of the great "captains of industry," does not tend to foster personal independence—the basis of all virtues—nor will it tend to preserve the characteristics which particularly have made Californians proud of their state.

Henry George asked what the railroad would bring, but not too many other people did. Many people would later ask whether it had served the common weal to transform the Sacramento and San Joaquin Valleys from a seasonal shallow sea to a protected hothouse requiring the annual application on each square mile of 3.87 tons of chemical pesticides, but not too many people asked this before the dams; those who did ask, for whatever reason, were categorized as "environmentalists," a word loosely used in this part of California to describe any perceived threat to the life of absolute personal freedom its citizens believe they lead. "California likes to be fooled," Cedar-

quist, the owner in *The Octopus* of a failed San Fran ironworks, advises Presley when they happen to me (where else?) the Bohemian Club. "Do you suppose grim [the Collis P. Huntington figure] could conver whole San Joaquin Valley into his back yard otherwise

"What the Railroad Will Bring Us" remained, my generation at least, routine assigned reading for C fornia children, one more piece of evidence that assig reading makes nothing happen. I used to think Henry George had overstated the role of the railroad, in one sense he had: the railroad, of course, was merely last stage of a process already underway, one that had basis in the character of the settlement, in the very qual recommended by "What the Railroad Will Bring Us" "a general hopefulness and self-reliance," or "a feeling personal independence or equality," or "the latent feelin of everyone that he might 'make a strike.'" This proces one of trading the state to outside owners in exchange fo their (it now seems) entirely temporary agreement t enrich us, in other words the pauperization of California had in fact begun at the time Americans first entered th state, took what they could, and, abetted by the nativ weakness for boosterism, set about selling the rest.

Josiah Royce understood this negative side of the California character, but persisted in what was for him the essential conviction that the California community was so positive a force as to correct its own character. He allowed that "a general sense of social irresponsibility is, even today, the average Californian's easiest failing." Still, he

Part Two

I

I N the May 1935 issue of the *American Mercury,*
William Faulkner published one of the few pieces of
fiction he set in California, a short story he called
"Golden Land." "Golden Land" deals with a day in the
life of Ira Ewing, Jr., age forty-eight, a man for whom
"twenty-five years of industry and desire, of shrewdness
and luck and even fortitude," seem recently to have come
to ashes. At fourteen, Ira Ewing had fled Nebraska on a
westbound freight. By the time he was thirty, he had
married the daughter of a Los Angeles carpenter, fathered
a son and a daughter, and secured a foothold in the real
estate business. By the time we meet him, eighteen years
later, he is in a position to spend fifty thousand dollars a
year, a sizable amount in 1935. He has been able to bring
his widowed mother from Nebraska and install her in a
house in Glendale. He has been able to provide for his
children "luxuries and advantages which his own father
not only could not have conceived in fact but would have
condemned completely in theory."

Yet nothing is working out. Ira's daughter, Samantha,
who wants to be in show business and has taken the name
"April Lalear," is testifying in a lurid trial reported on

page one ("April Lalear Bares Orgy Secrets") of the newspapers placed on the reading table next to Ira's bed. Ira, less bewildered than weary, tries not to look at the accompanying photographs of Samantha, the "hard, blonde, and inscrutable" daughter who "alternately stared back or flaunted long pale shins." Nor is Samantha the exclusive source of the leaden emptiness Ira now feels instead of hunger: there is also his son, Voyd, who continues to live at home but has not spoken unprompted to his father in two years, not since the morning when Voyd, drunk, was delivered home to his father wearing, "in place of underclothes, a woman's brassiere and step-ins."

Since Ira prides himself on being someone who will entertain no suggestion that his life is not the success that his business achievement would seem to him to promise, he discourages discussion of his domestic trials, and has tried to keep the newspapers featuring April Lalear and the orgy secrets away from his mother. Via the gardener, however, Ira's mother has learned about her granddaughter's testimony, and she is reminded of the warning she once gave her son, after she had seen Samantha and Voyd stealing cash from their mother's purse: "You make money too easy," she had told Ira. "This whole country is too easy for us Ewings. It may be all right for them that have been born here for generations, I don't know about that. But not for us."

"But these children were born here," Ira had said.

"Just one generation," his mother had said. "The generation before that they were born in a sod-roofed dugout on the Nebraska wheat frontier. And the one before that in a log house in Missouri. And the one before that in a Kentucky blockhouse with Indians around it. This world has never been easy for Ewings. Maybe the Lord never intended it to be."

"But it is from now on," the son had insisted. "For you and me too. But mostly for them."

"Golden Land" does not entirely hold up, nor, I would guess, will it ever be counted among the best Faulkner stories. Yet it retains, for certain Californians, a nagging resonance, and opens the familiar troubling questions. I grew up in a California family that derived, from the single circumstance of having been what Ira Ewing's mother called "born here for generations," considerable pride, much of it, it seemed to me later, strikingly unearned. "The trouble with these new people," I recall hearing again and again as a child in Sacramento, "is they think it's supposed to be easy." The phrase "these new people" generally signified people who had moved to California after World War Two, but was tacitly extended back to include the migration from the Dust Bowl during the 1930s, and often further. New people, we were given to understand, remained ignorant of our special history, insensible to the hardships endured to make it, blind not only to the dangers the place still presented but to the shared responsibilities its continued habitation demanded.

If my grandfather spotted a rattlesnake while driving, he would stop his car and go into the brush after it. To do less, he advised me more than once, was to endanger whoever later entered the brush, and so violate what he called "the code of the West." New people, I was told, did not understand their responsibility to kill rattlesnakes. Nor did new people understand that the water that came from the tap in, say, San Francisco, was there only because part of Yosemite had been flooded to put it there. New people did not understand the necessary dynamic of the fires, the seven-year cycles of flood and drought, the physical reality of the place. "Why didn't they go back to Truckee?" a young mining engineer from back East asked when my grandfather pointed out the site of the Donner Party's last encampment. I recall hearing this story repeatedly. I also recall the same grandfather, my mother's father, whose family had migrated from the hardscrabble Adirondack frontier in the eighteenth century to the hardscrabble Sierra Nevada foothills in the nineteenth, working himself up into writing an impassioned letter-to-the-editor over a fifth-grade textbook in which one of the illustrations summed up California history as a sunny progression from Spanish Señorita to Gold Miner to Golden Gate Bridge. What the illustration seemed to my grandfather to suggest was that those responsible for the textbook believed the settlement of California to have been "easy," history rewritten, as he saw it, for the new people. There were definite ambiguities in this: Ira Ewing and his children were, of course, new people, but so, less than a century before, had my grandfather's family been. New people could be seen, by people like my grandfather, as indifferent to everything that had made California work, but the ambiguity was this: new people were also who were making California rich.

Californians whose family ties to the state predate World War Two have an equivocal and often uneasy relationship to the postwar expansion. Joan Irvine Smith, whose family's eighty-eight-thousand-acre ranch in Orange County was developed during the 1960s, later created, on the twelfth floor of the McDonnell Douglas Building in Irvine, a city that did not exist before the Irvines developed their ranch, the Irvine Museum, dedicated to the California impressionist or plein air paintings she had begun collecting in 1991. "There is more nostalgia for me in these paintings than in actually going out to look at what used to be the ranch now that it has been developed, because I'm looking at what I looked at as a child," she told *Art in California* about this collection. Her attraction to the genre had begun, she said, when she was a child and would meet her stepfather for lunch at the California Club, where the few public rooms in which women were at that time allowed were decorated with California landscapes lent by the members. "I can look at those paintings and see what the ranch was as I remember it when I was a little girl."

The California Club, which is on Flower Street in downtown Los Angeles, was then and is still the heart of Southern California's old-line business establishment, the Los Angeles version of the Bohemian and Pacific Union Clubs in San Francisco. On any given day since

World War Two, virtually everyone lunching at the California Club, most particularly not excluding Joan Irvine, has had a direct or indirect investment in the development of California, which is to say in the obliteration of the undeveloped California on display at the Irvine Museum. In the seventy-four paintings chosen for inclusion in *Selections from the Irvine Museum,* the catalogue published by the museum to accompany a 1992 traveling exhibition, there are hills and desert and mesas and arroyos. There are mountains, coastline, big sky. There are stands of eucalyptus, sycamore, oak, cottonwood. There are washes of California poppies. As for fauna, there are, in the seventy-four paintings, three sulphur-crested cockatoos, one white peacock, two horses, and nine people, four of whom are dwarfed by the landscape and two of whom are indistinct Indians paddling a canoe.

Some of this is romantic (the indistinct Indians), some washed with a slightly falsified golden light, in the tradition that runs from Bierstadt's "lustrous, pearly mist" to the "Kinkade Glow." Most of these paintings, however, reflect the way the place actually looks, or looked, not only to Joan Irvine but also to me and to anyone else who knew it as recently as 1960. It is this close representation of a familiar yet vanished landscape that gives the Irvine collection its curious effect, that of a short-term memory misfire: these paintings hang in a city, Irvine (population more than one hundred and fifty thousand, with a University of California campus enrolling some nineteen thousand students), that was forty years ago a mirror image of the paintings themselves, bean fields and grazing, the heart but by no means all of the cattle and sheep operation amassed by the great-grandfather of the founder of the Irvine Museum.

The disposition of such a holding can be, for its inheritors, a fraught enterprise. "On the afternoon of his funeral we gathered to honor this man who had held such a legacy intact for the main part of his ninety-one years," Jane Hollister Wheelwright wrote in *The Ranch Papers* about the aftermath of her father's death and the prospect of being forced to sell the Hollister ranch. "All of us were deeply affected. Some were stunned by the prospect of loss; others gloated, contemplating cash and escape. We were bitterly divided, but none could deny the power of that land. The special, spiritually meaningful (and often destructive) impact of the ranch was obvious. I proved it by my behavior, as did the others."

That was 1961. Joan Irvine Smith had replaced her mother on the board of the Irvine Company four years before, in 1957, the year she was twenty-four. She had seen, a good deal more clearly and realistically than Jane Hollister Wheelwright would see four years later, the solution she wanted for her family's ranch, and she had seen the rest of the Irvine board as part of the problem: by making small deals, selling off bits of the whole, the board was nibbling away at the family's principal asset, the size of its holding. It was she who pressed the architect William Pereira to present a master plan. It was she who saw the potential return in giving the land for a University of California campus. It was she, most importantly, who insisted on maintaining an interest in the ranch's development. And, in the end, which meant after years of internecine battles and a series of litigations extending to 1991, it was she who more or less prevailed. In 1960, before the Irvine ranch was developed, there were 719,500 people in all of Orange County. In 2000 there were close to 3 million, most of whom would not have been there had two families, the Irvines in the central part of the county and the inheritors of Richard O'Neill's Rancho Santa Margarita and Mission Viejo acreage in the southern, not developed their ranches.

This has not been a case in which the rising tide floated all boats. Not all of Orange County's new residents came to realize what would have seemed the middle-class promise of its growth. Not all of those residents even had somewhere to live: some settled into the run-down motels built in the mid-1950s, at the time Disneyland opened, and were referred to locally, because they had nowhere else to live and could not afford the deposits required for apartment rental, as "motel people." In his 1986 *The New California: Facing the 21st Century,* the political columnist Dan Walters quoted *The Orange County Register* on motel people: "Mostly Anglo, they're the county's newest migrant workers: instead of picking grapes, they inspect semiconductors." This kind of week-by-week or even day-by-day living arrangement has taken hold in other parts of the country, but remains particularly entrenched in Southern California, where apartment rents rose to meet the increased demand from people priced out of a housing market in which even the least promising bungalow can sell for several hundred thousand dollars.

By the year 2000, according to *The Los Angeles Times,* some hundred Orange County motels were inhabited almost exclusively by the working poor, people who made, say, $280 a week sanding airplane parts, or $7 an hour at Disney's "California Adventure" park. "A land celebrating the richness and diversity of California, its natural resources, and pioneering spirit of its people," the web site for "California Adventure" read. "I can look at these paintings and look back," Joan Irvine Smith told *Art in California* about the collection she bought with the proceeds of looking exclusively, and to a famous degree, forward. "I can see California as it was and as we will never see it again." Hers is an extreme example of the conundrum that to one degree or another confronts any Californian who profited from the boom years: if we could still see California as it was, how many of us could now afford to see it?

2

What is the railroad to do for us?—this railroad that
we have looked for, hoped for, prayed for so long?

— Henry George,
"What the Railroad Will Bring Us"

LAKEWOOD, California, the Los Angeles County
community where in early 1993 an amorphous
high school clique identifying itself as the Spur
Posse achieved a short-lived national notoriety, lies between the Long Beach and San Gabriel Freeways, east of
the San Diego, part of that vast grid familiar to the casual
visitor mainly from the air, Southern California's industrial underbelly, the thousand square miles of aerospace
and oil that powered the place's apparently endless expansion. Like much of the southern end of this grid, Lakewood was until after World War Two agricultural, several
thousand acres of beans and sugar beets just inland from
the Signal Hill oil field and across the road from the plant

behind the Long Beach airport that the federal government completed in 1941 for Donald Douglas.

This Douglas plant, with the outsized American flag whipping in the wind and the huge forward-slanted letters *MCDONNELL DOUGLAS* wrapped around the building and the MD-11s parked like cars off Lakewood Boulevard, was at the time I first visited Lakewood in 1993 the single most noticeable feature on the local horizon, but for a while, not long after World War Two, there had been another: a hundred-foot pylon, its rotating beacon visible for several miles, erected to advertise the opening, in April 1950, of what was meant to be the world's biggest subdivision, a tract larger in conception than the original Long Island Levittown, 17,500 houses waiting to be built on the 3,400 dead-level acres that three California developers, Mark Taper and Ben Weingart and Louis Boyar, had purchased for $8.8 million from the Montana Land Company.

Lakewood, the sign read at the point on Lakewood Boulevard where Bellflower would become Lakewood, *Tomorrow's City Today.* What was offered for sale in Tomorrow's City, as in most subdivisions of the postwar period, was a raw lot and the promise of a house. Each of the 17,500 houses was to be 950 to 1,100 square feet on a fifty-by-hundred-foot lot. Each was to be a one-story stucco (seven floor plans, twenty-one different exteriors, no identical models to be built next to or facing each other) painted in one of thirty-nine color schemes. Each was to have oak floors, a glass-enclosed shower, a stainless-steel double sink, a garbage disposal unit, and either two or three bedrooms. Each was to sell for between eight and ten thousand dollars. *Low FHA, Vets No Down.* There were to be thirty-seven playgrounds, twenty schools. There were to be seventeen churches. There were to be 133 miles of street, paved with an inch and a half of No. 2 macadam on an aggregate base.

There was to be, and this was key not only to the project but to the nature of the community which eventually evolved, a regional shopping center, "Lakewood Center," which in turn was conceived as America's largest retail complex: 256 acres, parking for ten thousand cars, anchored by a May Company. "Lou Boyar pointed out that they would build a shopping center and around that a city, that he would make a city for us and millions for himself," John Todd, a resident of Lakewood since its beginning and later its city attorney, wrote of the planning stage. "Everything about this entire project was perfect," Mark Taper said in 1969, when he sat down with city officials to work up a local history. "Things happened that may never happen again."

What he meant, of course, was the perfect synergy of time and place, the seamless confluence of World War Two and the Korean War and the G.I. Bill and the defense contracts that began to flood Southern California as the Cold War set in. Here on this raw acreage on the flood plain between the Los Angeles and San Gabriel Rivers was where two powerfully conceived national interests, that of keeping the economic engine running and that of creating an enlarged middle or consumer class, could be seen to converge.

The scene beneath the hundred-foot pylon during that spring of 1950 was Cimarron: thirty thousand people showed up for the first day of selling. Twenty thousand showed up on weekends throughout the spring. Near the sales office was a nursery where children could be left while parents toured the seven completed and furnished model houses. Thirty-six salesmen worked day and evening shifts, showing potential buyers how their G.I. benefits, no down payment, and thirty years of monthly payments ranging from $43 to $54 could elevate them to ownership of a piece of the future. Deals were closed on 611 houses the first week. One week saw construction started on 567. A new foundation was excavated every fifteen minutes. Cement trucks were lined up for a mile, waiting to move down the new blocks pouring foundations. Shingles were fed to roofers by conveyer belt. And, at the very point when sales had begun to slow, as Taper recalled at the 1969 meeting with city officials, "the Korean War was like a new stimulation."

"There was this new city growing—growing like leaves," one of the original residents, who with her husband had opened a delicatessen in Lakewood Center, said when she was interviewed for an oral history project undertaken by the city and Lakewood High School. "So we decided this is where we should start. . . . There were young people, young children, schools, a young government that was just starting out. We felt all the big stores were coming in. May Company and all the other places started opening. So we rented one of the stores and we were in business." These World War Two and Korean War veterans and their wives who started out in Lakewood were, typically, about thirty years old. They were, typically, not from California but from the Midwest and the border South. They were, typically, blue-collar and lower-level white collar. They had 1.7 children, they had steady jobs. Their experience tended to reinforce the conviction that social and economic mobility worked exclusively upward.

Donald J. Waldie, while he was working as the City of Lakewood's public information officer, wrote an extraordinary book, *Holy Land: A Suburban Memoir,* published in 1996, a series of interconnected essays about someone who, like their author, lived in Lakewood and worked at City Hall. "Naively, you could say that Lakewood was the American dream made affordable for a generation of industrial workers who in the preceding generation could never aspire to that kind of ownership," he said one morning when we were talking about the way the place was developed. "They were fairly but not entirely homogenous in their ethnic background. They were oriented to aerospace. They worked for Hughes, they worked for Douglas, they worked at the naval station and shipyard in Long Beach. They worked, in other words, at all the places that exemplified the bright future that California was supposed to be."

Donald Waldie grew up in Lakewood, and, after Cal State Long Beach and graduate work at the University of California at Irvine, had chosen to come back, as had a striking number of people who lived there. In a county increasingly populated by low-income Mexican and Central American and Asian immigrants and pressed by the continuing needs of its low-income blacks, almost sixty thousand of Lakewood's seventy-some thousand citizens were still, in the spring of 1993, white. More than half had been born in California, and most of the rest in the Midwest and the South. The largest number of those employed worked, just as their fathers and grandfathers had, for Douglas or Hughes or Rockwell or the Long Beach naval station and shipyard or for the many subcontractors and vendors that did business with Douglas and Hughes and Rockwell and the Long Beach naval station and shipyard.

People who lived in Lakewood did not necessarily think of themselves as living in Los Angeles, and could often list the occasions on which they had visited there, to see the Dodgers play, say, or to show a relative from out of state the Music Center. Their apprehension of urban woes remained remote: the number of homeless people in Lakewood either in shelters or "visible on street," according to the 1990 Census, was zero. When residents of Lakewood spoke about the rioting that had begun in Los Angeles after the 1992 Rodney King verdicts, they were talking about events that seemed to them, despite the significant incidence of arson and looting in such neighboring communities as Long Beach and Compton, to have occurred somewhere else. "We're far away from that element," one woman to whom I spoke said when the subject of the riots came up. "If you've driven around . . ."

"Little suburbia," a neighbor said.

"America U.S.A., right here."

The neighbor's husband worked at a nearby Rockwell plant, not the Rockwell plant in Lakewood. The Rockwell plant in Lakewood had closed in 1992, a thousand jobs gone. The scheduled closing of the Long Beach naval station would mean almost nine thousand jobs gone. The Federal Base Closure and Realignment Commission had granted a provisional stay to the Long Beach naval shipyard, which adjoined the naval station and employed another four thousand people, but its prospects for survival remained dim. One thing that was not remote in Lakewood in 1993, one thing so close that not many people even wanted to talk about it, was the apprehension that what had already happened to the Rockwell plant and would happen to the Long Beach naval station and shipyard could also happen to the Douglas plant. I recall talking one day to Carl Cohn, then superintendent of the Long Beach Unified School District, which included Lakewood. "There's a tremendous fear that at some point this operation might go away entirely," he said. "I mean that's kind of one of the whispered things around town. Nobody wants it out there."

Douglas had already, in 1993, moved part of its MD-80 production to Salt Lake City. Douglas had already moved part of what remained of its C-17 production to St. Louis. Douglas had already moved the T-45 to St. Louis. In a 1992 study called *Impact of Defense Cuts on California,* the California Commission on State Finance had estimated nineteen thousand layoffs still to come from Hughes and McDonnell Douglas, but by 1992 there had already been, in Southern California, some twenty-one thousand McDonnell Douglas layoffs. According to a June 1993 report on aerospace unemployment prepared by researchers at the UCLA School of Architecture and Urban Planning, half the California aerospace workers laid off in 1989 were, two years later, either still unemployed or no longer living in California. Most of those who did find jobs had ended up in lower-income service jobs; only seventeen percent had gone back to work in the aerospace industry at figures approaching their original salaries. Of those laid off in 1991 and 1992, only sixteen percent, a year later, had found jobs of any kind.

It was the Douglas plant on the Lakewood city line, the one with the flag whipping in the wind and the logo wrapped around the building, that had by 1993 taken the hit for almost eighteen thousand of McDonnell Douglas's twenty-one thousand layoffs. "I've got two kids, a first and a third grader," Carl Cohn told me. "When you take your kid to a birthday party and your wife starts talking about so-and-so's father just being laid off—there are all kinds of implications, including what's going to be spent on a kid's birthday party. These concrete things really come home to you. And you realize, yeah, this bad economic situation is very real." The message on the marquee at Rochelle's Restaurant and Motel and Convention Center, between Douglas and the Long Beach airport, still read "Welcome Douglas Happy Hour 4–7," but the place was nailed shut, a door banging in the wind. "We've developed good citizens," Mark Taper said about Lakewood in 1969. "Enthusiastic owners of property. Owners of a piece of their country—a stake in the land." This was a sturdy but finally unsupportable ambition, sustained for forty years by good times and the good will of the federal government.

When people in Lakewood spoke about what they called "Spur," or "the situation at the high school," some meant the series of allegations that had led to the March 1993 arrests—with requests that charges be brought on ten counts of rape by intimidation, four counts of unlawful sexual intercourse, one count of forcible rape, one count of oral copulation, and one count of lewd conduct with a minor under the age of fourteen— of nine current or former Lakewood High School students who either happened to be or were believed to be members of an informal fraternity known locally as the Spur Posse. Others meant not the allegations, which they saw as either outright inventions or representations of events open to interpretation (the phrase "consensual sex" got heavy usage), but rather the national attention that followed those allegations, the invasion of Lakewood by what its residents called "you people," or "you folks," or "the media," and the appearance, on *Jenny Jones* and *Jane Whitney* and *Maury Povich* and *Nightline* and *Montel Williams* and *Dateline* and *Donahue* and *The Home Show,* of two hostile and briefly empowered arrangements of hormones, otherwise known as "the boys" and "the girls."

For a moment that spring they had seemed to be on view everywhere, those blank-faced Lakewood girls, those feral Lakewood boys. There were the dead eyes, the thick

necks, the jaws that closed only to chew gum. There was
the refusal or inability to process the simplest statement
without rephrasing it. There was the fuzzy relationship to
language, the tendency to seize on a drifting fragment of
something once heard and repeat it, not quite get it right,
worry it like a bone. The news that some schools distributed condoms had been seized in mid-drift, for example,
and pressed into service as an extenuating circumstance,
the fact that Lakewood High School had never distributed
condoms notwithstanding. "The schools, they're handing
out condoms and stuff like that, and like, if they're handing out condoms, why don't they tell us you can be
arrested for it?" one Spur asked Gary Collins and Sarah
Purcell on *The Home Show.* "They pass out condoms, teach
sex education and pregnancy this, pregnancy that, but
they don't teach us any rules," another told Jane Gross of
The New York Times. "Schools hand out condoms, teach
safe sex," the mother of a Spur complained on *The Home
Show.* "It's the society, they have these clinics, they have
abortions, they don't have to tell their parents, the schools
give out condoms, jeez, what does that tell you?" the
father of one Lakewood boy, a sixteen-year-old who had
just admitted to a juvenile-court petition charging him
with lewd conduct with a ten-year-old girl, asked a television interviewer. "I think people are blowing this thing
way out of proportion," David Ferrell of *The Los Angeles
Times* was told by one Spur. "It's all been blown out of proportion as far as I'm concerned," he was told by another.
"Of course there were several other sex scandals at the
time, so this perfectly normal story got blown out of

proportion," I was told by a Spur parent. "People, you know, kind of blow it all out of proportion," a Spur advised viewers of *Jane Whitney.* "They blow it out of proportion a lot," another said on the same show. A Spur girlfriend, "Jodi," called in to offer her opinion: "I think it's been blown way out of proportion, like way out of proportion."

Each of these speakers seemed to be referring to a cultural misery apprehended only recently, and then dimly. Those who mentioned "blowing it out of proportion" were complaining specifically about "the media," and its "power," but more generally about a sense of being besieged, set upon, at the mercy of forces beyond local control. "The whole society has changed," one Spur parent told me. "Morals have changed. Girls have changed. It used to be, girls would be more or less the ones in control. Girls would hold out, girls would want to be married at eighteen or nineteen and they'd keep their sights on having a home and love and a family." What seemed most perplexing to these Lakewood residents was that the disruption was occurring in what they uniformly referred to as "a middle-class community like this one," or sometimes "an upper-middle-class community like this one." "We're an upper-middle-class community," I was told one morning outside the Los Padrinos Juvenile Court in Downey, where a group of Lakewood women were protesting the decision of the Los Angeles County district attorney's office not to bring most of the so-called "sex charges" requested by the sheriff's department. *"It Wasn't The Bloods, Crips, Longos, It Was The Spurs,"* the hand-lettered signs read that morning, "the Longos" being a Long Beach gang. "*What If One of the Victims Had Been Your Grand-daughter, Huh, Mr. District Attorney?*" "It's a very hush-hush community," another protester said. "Very low profile, they don't want to make waves, don't want to step on anybody's toes." The following is an extract from the first page of Donald J. Waldie's *Holy Land: A Suburban Memoir:*

> He knew his suburb's first 17,500 houses had been built in less than three years. He knew what this must have cost, but he did not care.
>
> The houses still worked.
>
> He thought of them as middle class even though 1,100-square-foot tract houses on streets meeting at right angles are not middle class at all.
>
> Middle-class houses are the homes of people who would not live here.

This is in fact the tacit dissonance at the center of every moment in Lakewood, which is why the average day there raises, for the visitor, so many and such vertiginous questions:

What does it cost to create and maintain an artificial ownership class?

Who pays?

Who benefits?

What happens when that class stops being useful?

What does it mean to drop back below the line?

What does it cost to hang on above it, how do you

behave, what do you say, what are the pitons you drive into the granite?

One of the ugliest and most revelatory of the many ugly and revelatory moments that characterized the 1993 television appearances of Lakewood's Spur Posse members occurred on *Jane Whitney,* when a nineteen-year-old Lakewood High School graduate named Chris Albert ("Boasts He Has 44 'Points' For Having Sex With Girls") turned mean with a member of the audience, a young black woman who had tried to suggest that the Spurs on view were not exhibiting what she considered native intelligence.

"I don't get—I don't understand what she's saying," Chris Albert had at first said, letting his jaw go slack as these boys tended to do when confronted with an unwelcome, or in fact any, idea.

Another Spur had interpreted: "We're dumb. She's saying we're dumb."

"What education does she have?" Chris Albert had then demanded, and crouched forward toward the young woman, as if trying to shake himself alert. "Where do you work at? McDonald's? Burger King?" A third Spur had tried to interrupt, but Chris Albert, once roused, could not be deflected. "Five twenty-five?" he said. "Five fifty?" And then, there it was, the piton, driven in this case not into granite but into shale, already disintegrating: *"I go to college."* Two years later Chris Albert would be dead, shot in the chest and killed during a Fourth of July celebration on the Pacific Coast Highway in Huntington Beach.

3

L A K E W O O D exists because at a given time in a different economy it had seemed an efficient idea to provide population density for the mall and a labor pool for the Douglas plant. There are a lot of towns like Lakewood in California. They were California's mill towns, breeder towns for the boom. When times were good and there was money to spread around, these were the towns that proved Marx wrong, that managed to increase the proletariat and simultaneously, by calling it middle class, to co-opt it. Such towns were organized around the sedative idealization of team sports, which were believed to develop "good citizens," and therefore tended to the idealization of adolescent males. During the good years, the years for which places like Lakewood or Canoga Park or El Segundo or Pico Rivera existed, the preferred resident was in fact an adolescent or post-adolescent male, ideally one already married and mortgaged, in harness to the plant, a good worker, a steady consumer, a team player, someone who played ball, a good citizen.

When towns like these came on hard times, it was the same adolescent males, only recently the community's most valued asset, who were most visibly left with nowhere to go. Among the Spur Posse members who appeared on the talk shows that spring, a striking number had been out of high school a year, or even two years, but did not seem actively engaged in a next step. "It was some of the older kids who were so obnoxious, so arrogant," one Spur father, Donald Belman, told me. "They're the ones who were setting up talk-show appearances just for the money. I had to kick them out of my house, they were answering my phone, monitoring my mail. They were just in it for the money, quick cash." Jane Gross of *The New York Times* asked one of these postgraduate Spurs what he had been doing since high school. "Partying," he said. "Playing ball."

Good citizens were encouraged, when partying failed, when playing ball failed, when they finally noticed that the jobs had gone to Salt Lake or St. Louis, to see their problem as one caused by "the media," or by "condoms in the schools," or by less-good citizens, or non-citizens. "Orange County is using illegal aliens now as a smoke-screen, as a scapegoat, because that's the way we get the white lower-income people to jump on board and say the immigrants are the problem," the wife of an aerospace engineer in Costa Mesa told Robert Scheer of *The Los Angeles Times*. "But we had our class differences before the immigrants. One of our sons was on the football team in the high school in Costa Mesa about twelve years ago. They had a great team and they were beating the pants off one of the schools in Newport Beach and the Newport stands started to cheer. *'Hey, hey, that's OK, you're gonna work for us one day.'*"

This is what it costs to create and maintain an artificial ownership class.

This is what happens when that class stops being useful.

Most adults to whom I spoke in Lakewood during that spring of 1993 shared a sense that something in town had gone wrong. Many connected this apprehension to the Spur Posse, or at least to certain Spur Posse members who had emerged, even before the arrests and for a variety of reasons, as the community's most visible males. Almost everyone agreed that this was a town in which what had been considered the definition of good parenting, the encouragement of assertive behavior among male children, had for some reason gotten badly out of hand. The point on which many people disagreed was whether sex was at the center of this problem, and some of these people felt troubled and misrepresented by the fact that public discussion of the situation in Lakewood had tended to focus exclusively on what they called "the sex charges," or "the sexual charges." "People have to understand," I was told by one plaintive mother. "This isn't about the sexual charges." Some believed the charges intrinsically unprovable. Others seemed simply to regard sex among teenagers as a combat zone with its own rules, a contained conflict from which they were prepared, as the district attorney was, to look away. Many seemed unaware of the extent to which questions of gender had come to occupy the nation's official attention, and so had failed to appreciate the ease with which the events in Lakewood could feed seamlessly into a discussion already in progress, offer a fresh context in which to recap Tailhook, Packwood, Anita Hill.

What happened that spring had begun, most people agreed, at least a year before, maybe more. Much of what got talked about had seemed, at first, suggestive mainly of underemployed teenagers playing at acting street. There had been threats, bully tactics, the systematic harassment of girls or younger children who made complaints or "stood up to" or in any way resisted the whim of a certain group of boys. Young children in Lakewood had come to know among themselves who to avoid in those thirty-seven playgrounds, what cars to watch for on those 133 miles of No. 2 macadam. "I'm talking about throughout the community," I was told by Karin Polacheck, who represented Lakewood on the board of education for the Long Beach Unified School District. "At the baseball fields, at the parks, at the markets, on the corners of schoolgrounds. They were organized enough that young children would say, 'Watch out for that car when it comes around,' 'Watch out for those boys.' I've heard stories of walking up and stealing baseball bats and telling kids, 'If you tell anyone I'll beat your head in.' I'm talking about young children, nine, ten years old. It's a small community. Younger kids knew that these older kids were out there."

"You're dead," the older boys would reportedly say, or "You're gonna get fucked up." "You're gonna get it." "You're gonna die." "I don't like who she's hanging with, why don't we just kill her now." There was a particular form of street terror mentioned by many people: invasive vehicular maneuvers construed by the targets as attempts to "run people down." "There were skid marks outside my house," one mother told me. "They were trying to scare my daughter. Her life was hell. She had chili-cheese nachos thrown at her at school." "They just like to intimidate people," I was repeatedly told. "They stare back at you. They don't go to school, they ditch. They ditch and then they beg the teacher to pass them, because they have to have a C average to play on the teams." "They came to our house in a truck to do something to my sister," one young woman told me. "She can't go anywhere. Can't even go to Taco Bell any more. Can't go to Jack-in-the-Box. They'll jump you. They followed me home not long ago, I just headed for the sheriff's office."

There had also been more substantive incidents, occurrences that could not be written off to schoolyard exaggeration or adolescent oversensitivity. There had been assaults in local parks, bicycles stolen and sold. There had been burglaries, credit cards and jewelry missing from the bedroom drawers of houses where local girls had been babysitting. There had even been, beginning in the summer of 1992, felony arrests: Donald Belman's son Dana, who was generally said to have "founded" the Spur Posse, was arrested on suspicion of stealing a certain number of guns from the bedroom of a house where he was said to have attended a party. Not long before that, in Las Vegas, Dana Belman and another Spur, Christopher Russo, had been detained for possession of stolen credit cards. Just before Christmas 1992, Dana Belman and Christopher

Russo were detained yet again, and arrested for alleged check forgery.

There were odd quirks here, details not entirely consistent with the community's preferred view of itself. There were the high school trips to Vegas and to Laughlin, which is a Nevada casino town on the Colorado River below Las Vegas. There was the question of the certain number of guns Dana Belman was suspected of having stolen from the bedroom of the house where he was said to have attended the party: the number of guns mentioned was nineteen. Still, these details seemed to go unremarked upon, and the events unconnected. People who had been targeted by the older boys believed themselves, they said later, "all alone in this." They believed that each occasion of harassment was discrete, unique. They did not yet see a pattern in the various incidents and felonies. They had not yet made certain inductive leaps. That was before the pipe bomb.

The pipe bomb exploded on the front porch of a house not far from Lakewood High School between three and three-thirty on the morning of February 12, 1993. It destroyed one porch support. It tore holes in the stucco. It threw shrapnel into parked cars. One woman remembered that her husband was working the night shift at Rockwell and she had been sleeping light as usual when the explosion woke her. The next morning she asked a neighbor if she had heard the noise. "And she said, 'You're not going to believe it when I tell you what that was.' And she explained to me that a pipe bomb had blown up on someone's front porch. And that it had been a gang retaliatory thing. 'Gang thing?' I said. 'What are you *talking* about, a gang thing?' And she said, 'Well, you know, Spur Posse.' And I said, 'Spur Posse, what *is* Spur Posse?'"

This was the point at which the principal of Lakewood High School and the local sheriff's office, which had been trying to get a handle on the rash of felonies around town, decided to ask certain parents to attend a special meeting at the high school. Letters were sent to twenty-five families, each of which was believed to have at least one Spur Posse son. Only some fifteen people showed up at the March 2 meeting. Sheriff's deputies from both the local station and the arson-explosives detail spoke. The cause for concern, as the deputies then saw it, was that the trouble, whatever it was, seemed to be escalating: first the felonies, then a couple of car cherry bombs without much damage, now this eight-inch pipe bomb, which appeared to have been directed at one or more Spur Posse members and had been, according to a member of the arson-explosives detail, "intended to kill." It was during this meeting that someone, it was hard to sort out who, said the word "rape." Most people to whom I talked at first said that the issue had been raised by one of the parents, but those who said this had not actually been present at the meeting. Asking about this after the fact tended to be construed as potentially hostile, because the Los Angeles attorney Gloria Allred, a specialist in high-profile gender cases, had by then appeared on the scene, giving press conferences, doing talk shows, talking about possible civil litigation on behalf of the six girls who had become her clients, and generally making people in Lakewood a little sensitive about who knew what and when they had known it and what they had done about what they knew.

What happened next was also unclear. Lakewood High School students recalled investigators from the sheriff's Whittier-based sex-abuse unit coming to the school, calling people in, questioning anyone who had even been seen talking to boys who were said to be Spurs. "I think they came up with a lot of wannabe boys," one mother told me. "Boys who wanted to belong to something that had notoriety to it." The presence of the investigators at the school might well have suggested that arrests could be pending, but school authorities said that they knew nothing until the morning of March 18, when sheriff's deputies appeared in the principal's office and said that they were going into classrooms to take boys out in custody. "There was never any allegation that any of these incidents took place on school ground or at school events or going to and from school," Carl Cohn said on the morning we talked in his Long Beach Unified School District office. He had not been present the morning the boys were taken from their classrooms in cutoffs and handcuffs, but the television vans had been, as had *The Los Angeles Times* and *The Long Beach Press-Telegram*. "Arresting the youngsters at school might have been convenient, but it very much contributed to what is now this media circus," he said. "The sheriff's department had a press briefing. Downtown. Los Angeles. Where they notified the media that they were going in. All you have to do is mention that the perpetrators are students at a particular school and everybody gets on the freeway."

The boys arrested were detained for four nights. All but one sixteen-year-old, who was charged with lewd conduct against a ten-year-old girl, were released without charges. When those still enrolled at Lakewood High went back to school, they were greeted with cheers by some students. "Of *course* they were treated as heroes, they'd been wrongly accused," I was told by Donald Belman, whose youngest son, Kristopher, was one of those arrested and released. "These girls pre-planned these things. They wanted to be looked on favorably, they wanted to be part of the clique. They wanted to be, hopefully, the girlfriends of these studs on campus." The Belman family celebrated Kristopher's release by going out for hamburgers at McDonald's, which was, Donald Belman told *The Los Angeles Times,* "the American way."

Some weeks later the district attorney's office released a statement which read in part: "After completing an extensive investigation and analysis of the evidence, our conclusion is that there is no credible evidence of forcible rape involving any of these boys. . . . Although there is evidence of unlawful sexual intercourse, it is the policy of this office not to file criminal charges where there is consensual sex among teenagers. . . . The arrogance and contempt for young women which have been displayed, while appalling, cannot form the basis for criminal charges." "The district attorney on this did her homework," Donald Belman told me. "She questioned all these kids, she found

out these girls weren't the victims they were made out to
be. One of these girls had tattoos for chrissake." "If it's
true about the ten-year-old, I feel bad for her and her family," one Spur told David Ferrell of *The Los Angeles Times*.
"My regards go out to the family." As far as Lakewood
High was concerned, it was time to begin, its principal
said, "the healing process."

D onald and Dottie Belman, at the time they became
the most public of the Spur Posse parents, had lived
for twenty-two of their twenty-five years of marriage in a
beige stucco house on Greentop Street in Lakewood. Donald Belman, who worked as a salesman for an aerospace
vendor, selling to the large machine shops and to prime
contractors like Douglas, had graduated in 1963 from
Lakewood High School, spent four years in the Marine
Corps, and come home to start a life with Dottie, herself a
1967 Lakewood High graduate. "I held out for that white
dress," Dottie Belman told Janet Wiscombe of *The Long
Beach Press-Telegram*. "The word 'sex' was never spoken in
my home. People in movies went into the bedroom and
closed the door and came out with a smile on their face.
Now people are having brutal sex on TV. They aren't
making love. There is nothing romantic about it."

This was a family that had been, by its own and other
accounts, intensively focused on its three sons, Billy, then
twenty-three, Dana, twenty, and Kristopher, eighteen,
all of whom, at that time, still lived at home. "I'd hate
to have my kids away from me for two or three days in

Chicago or New York," Donald Belman told me by way of explaining why he had given his imprimatur to the appearance of his two younger sons on *The Home Show,* which was shot in Los Angeles, but not initially on *Jenny Jones,* which was shot in Chicago. "All these talk shows start calling, I said, 'Don't do it. They're just going to lie about you, they're going to set you up.' The more the boys said no, the more the shows enticed them. *The Home Show* was where I relented. They were offering a thousand dollars and a limo and it was in L.A. *Jenny Jones* offered I think fifteen hundred, but they'd have to fly."

During the years before this kind of guidance was needed, Donald Belman was always available to coach the boys' teams. There had been Park League, there had been Little League. There had been Pony League, Colt League, Pop Warner. Dottie Belman had regularly served as Team Mother, and remembered literally running from her job as a hairdresser so that she could have dinner on the table every afternoon at five-fifteen. "They would make a home run or a touchdown and I held my head high," she told the *Press-Telegram.* "We were reliving our past. We'd walk into Little League and we were hot stuff. I'd go to Von's and people would come up to me and say, 'Your kids are great.' I was so proud. Now I go to Von's at five a.m. in disguise. I've been Mother of the Year. I've sacrificed everything for my kids. Now I feel like I have to defend my honor."

The youngest Belman, Kristopher, who graduated from Lakewood High in June 1993, had been one of the boys arrested and released without charges that March. "I was crazy that weekend," his father told me. "My boy's in jail, Kris, he's never been in any trouble whatsoever, he's an average student, a star athlete. He doesn't even have to be in school, he has enough credits to graduate, you don't have to stay in school after you're eighteen. But he's there. Just to be with his friends." Around the time of graduation, Kristopher was arraigned on a charge of "forcible lewd conduct" based on an alleged 1989 incident involving a girl who was then thirteen; this charge was later dropped and Kristopher Belman agreed to do one hundred hours of community service. The oldest Belman son, Billy, according to his father, was working and going to school. The middle son, Dana, had graduated from Lakewood High in 1991 and had been named, as his father and virtually everyone else who mentioned him pointed out, "Performer of the Year 1991," for wrestling, in the Lakewood Youth Sports Hall of Fame. The Lakewood Youth Sports Hall of Fame is not at the high school, not at City Hall, but in a McDonald's, at the corner of Woodruff and Del Amo. "They're all standouts athletically," Donald Belman told me. "My psychology and philosophy is this: I'm a standup guy, I love my sons, I'm proud of their accomplishments." Dana, his father said, was at that time "looking for work," a quest complicated by the thirteen felony burglary and forgery charges on which he was then awaiting trial.

Dottie Belman, who had cancer surgery in April 1993, had filed for divorce in 1992 but for a year continued to live with her husband and sons on Greentop Street. "If Dottie wants to start a new life, I'm not going to hold her back," Donald Belman told the *Press-Telegram*. "I'm a solid guy. Just a solid citizen. I see no reason for any thought that our family isn't just all-American, basic and down-to-earth." Dottie Belman, when she spoke to the *Press-Telegram,* had been more reflective. "The wrecking ball shot right through the mantel and the house has crumbled," she said. "Dana said the other day, 'I want to be in the ninth grade again, and I want to do everything differently. I had it all. I was Mr. Lakewood. I was a star. I was popular. As soon as I graduated, I lost the recognition. I want to go back to the wonderful days. Now it's one disaster after another.'"

"You saw the papers," Ira Ewing says in "Golden Land" to the woman, a divorcée with a fourteen-year-old child of her own, who has become his sole consolation. "I can't understand it! After all the advantages that . . . after all I tried to do for them—"

The woman tries to calm him, offers him lunch.

"No. I don't want any lunch.—After all I have tried to give—"

Which was another way of saying: "The wrecking ball shot right through the mantel and the house has crumbled." It was 1996 when Dana Belman, convicted on three counts of burglary in the first degree, began serving a ten-year sentence at the California Men's Colony in San Luis Obispo. It was 1999 when he was discharged from prison, and a year later when he was released from parole.

4

ONCE when I was twelve or thirteen and had
checked the Lynds' *Middletown* and *Middletown in
Transition* out of the Sacramento library, I asked
my mother to what "class" we belonged.

"It's not a word we use," she said. "It's not the way we
think."

On one level I believed this to be a willful misreading
of what even a twelve-year-old could see to be the
situation and on another level I understood it to be true:
it was not the way we thought in California. We believed
in fresh starts. We believed in good luck. We believed in
the miner who scratched together one last stake and
struck the Comstock Lode. We believed in the wildcatter
who leased arid land at two and a half cents an acre and
brought in Kettleman Hills, fourteen million barrels
of crude in its first three years. We believed in all
the ways that apparently played-out possibilities could
while we slept turn green and golden. *Keep California
Green and Golden,* was the state's Smokey the Bear fire
motto around the time I was reading the Lynds. Put out
your campfire, kill the rattlesnake and watch the money
flow in.

And it did.

Even if it was somebody else's money.

The extent to which the postwar boom years confirmed this warp in the California imagination, and
in the expectations of its citizens, would be hard to overes-
timate. Good times today and better times tomorrow
were supposed to come with the territory, roll in with the
regularity of the breakers on what was once the coast of
the Irvine ranch and became Newport Beach, Balboa, Lido
Isle. Good times were the core conviction of the place, and
it was their only gradually apparent absence, in the early
1990s, that began to unsettle California in ways that no
one exactly wanted to plumb. The recognition that the
trend was no longer reliably up came late and hard to
California. The 1987 market crash was widely if not
consciously seen by its citizens as just one more of the
problems that plagued the America they had left behind,
evidence of a tiresome eastern negativity that would not
travel. Even when the defense plants started closing down
off the San Diego Freeway and the for-lease signs started
going up in Orange County, very few people wanted to
see a connection with the way life was going to be lived in
the California that was not immediately identifiable as
"aircraft."

This was in fact a state in which virtually every county
was to one degree or another dependent on defense contracts, from the billions upon billions of federal dollars
that flowed into Los Angeles County to the five-digit

contracts in counties like Plumas and Tehama and Tuolomne, yet the sheer geographical isolation of different parts of the state tended to obscure the elementary fact of its interrelatedness. Even within Los Angeles County, there had seemed no meaningful understanding that if General Motors shut down its assembly plant in Van Nuys, say, as it did in fact do in 1992, twenty-six hundred jobs lost, the bell would eventually toll in Bel Air, where the people lived who held the paper on the people who held the mortgages in Van Nuys. I recall asking a real estate broker on the west side of Los Angeles, in June 1988, what effect a defense cutback would have on the residential real estate boom then in progress. She said that such a cutback would have no effect on the west side of Los Angeles, because people who worked for Hughes and Douglas did not live in Pacific Palisades or Santa Monica or Malibu or Beverly Hills or Bel Air or Brentwood or Holmby Hills. "They live in Torrance maybe, or Canoga Park or somewhere."

Torrance is off the San Diego Freeway, west of Lakewood and south of El Segundo and Hawthorne and Lawndale and Gardena. Canoga Park is in the San Fernando Valley. People who worked for Hughes did in 1988 live in Torrance and Canoga Park. Five years later, after passage by the Arizona state legislature of a piece of tax-incentive legislation known locally as "the Hughes bill," Hughes was moving a good part of its El Segundo and Canoga Park operations to Tucson, and a well-known residential real estate broker on the west side of Los Angeles was advising clients that the market in Beverly Hills was down 47.5 percent. I remember being told, by virtually everyone to whom I spoke in Los Angeles during the few months that followed the 1992 riot, how much the riot had "changed" the city. Most of those who said this had lived in Los Angeles, as I had, during the 1965 Watts riot, but 1992, they assured me, had been "different," 1992 had "changed everything." The words they used seemed overfreighted, ominous in an unspecific way, words like "sad" and "bad." Since these were largely not people who had needed a riot to tell them that a volatile difference of circumstance and understanding existed between the city's haves and its have-nots, what they said puzzled me, and I pressed for a closer description of how Los Angeles had changed. After the riot, I was told, it was impossible to sell a house in Los Angeles. The notion it might have been impossible to sell a house in Los Angeles that year for a simpler reason, the reason being that the money had gone away, was still in 1992 so against the grain of the place as to be largely rejected.

The sad, bad times had actually begun, most people later allowed, in 1989, when virtually every defense contractor in Southern California began laying off. TRW had already dropped a thousand jobs. Rockwell had dropped five thousand as its B-1 program ended. Northrop dropped three thousand. Hughes dropped six thousand. Lockheed's union membership had declined, between 1981 and 1989, from fifteen thousand to seven thousand. McDonnell Douglas asked five thousand managers to resign, then to compete against one another for 2,900 jobs. Yet there was still, in McDonnell Douglas towns like Long Beach and Lakewood, space to maneuver, space for a little reflexive optimism and maybe even a trip to Vegas or Laughlin, since the parent corporation's Douglas Aircraft Company, the entity responsible for commercial as opposed to defense aircraft, was hiring for what was then its new MD-11 line. "Douglas is going great guns right now because of the commercial sector," I had been told in 1989 by David Hensley, who then headed the UCLA Business Forecasting Project. "Airline traffic escalated tremendously after deregulation. They're all beefing up their fleets, buying planes, which means Boeing up in Washington and Douglas here. That's a buffer against the downturn in defense spending."

These early defense layoffs were described at the time as "correctives" to the buildup of the Reagan years. Later they became "reorganizations" or "consolidations," words that still suggested the normal trimming and tacking of individual companies; the acknowledgment that the entire aerospace industry might be in trouble did not enter the language until a few years later, when "the restructuring" became preferred usage. The language used, like the geography, had worked to encyst the problem in certain communities, enabling Los Angeles at large to see the layoffs as abstractions, the predictable if difficult detritus of geopolitical change, in no way logically connected to whether the mini-mall at the corner made it or went under. It had been August 1990 before anybody much noticed that the commercial and residential real estate markets had dried up in Los Angeles. It had been October 1990 before a *Los Angeles Times* business report tentatively suggested that a local slowdown "appears to have begun."

Before 1991 ended, California had lost sixty thousand aerospace jobs. Many of these jobs had moved to southern and southwestern states offering lower salary scales, fewer regulations, and state and local governments, as in Arizona, not averse to granting tax incentives. Rockwell was entertaining bids on its El Segundo plant. Lockheed had decided to move production on its Advanced Tactical Fighter from Burbank to Marietta, Georgia. By 1992, more than seven hundred manufacturing plants had relocated or chosen to expand outside California, taking with them 107,000 jobs. Dun & Bradstreet reported 9,985 California business failures during the first six months of 1992. Analysts spoke approvingly of the transition from large companies to small businesses. *The Los Angeles Daily News* noted the "trend toward a new, more independent work force that will become less reliant on the company to provide for them and more inclined toward entrepreneurship," in other words, no benefits and no fixed salary, a recipe for motel people. Early in 1991, the Arco oil refinery in Carson, near where the Harbor and San Diego Freeways intersect, had placed advertisements in *The Los Angeles Times* and *The Orange County Register* for twenty-eight jobs paying $11.42 to $17.45 an hour. By the end of a week some fourteen thousand applicants had appeared in person at the refinery, and an unspecified number more had mailed in resumes. "I couldn't get in the front gate," an Arco spokesman told the *Times*. "Security people were directing traffic. It was quite a sight to see."

According to the Commission on State Finance in Sacramento, which monitors federal spending and its impact on the state, some 800,000 jobs were lost in California between 1988 and 1993. More than half the jobs lost were in Los Angeles County. The commission's May 1993 report estimated the further loss, between 1993 and 1997, of another 90,000 aerospace jobs, as well as 35,000 civilian jobs at bases scheduled for closure, but warned that "the potential loss could be greater if the defense industry continues to consolidate operations outside California." The Bank of America estimated six to eight hundred thousand jobs lost between 1990 and 1993, but made an even more bleak projection: four to five hundred thousand more jobs lost, in the state's "downsizing industries," between 1993 and 1995. This was what people in Los Angeles were talking about when they talked about the 1992 riot.

5

PEOPLE who worked on the line in the big California aerospace plants had constituted, in the good years, a kind of family. Many of them were second generation, and would mention the father who worked on the Snark missile, the brother who was foreman of a fabricating shop in Pico Rivera, the uncle who used to get what seemed like half the A-4 line out to watch Little League. These people might move among the half dozen or so major suppliers, but almost never outside them. The conventions of the marketplace remained alien to them. They worked to military specifications, or "milspec," a system that, *The Washington Post* noted, provided fifteen pages of specs for the making of chocolate cookies. They took considerable pride in working in an industry where decisions were not made in what Kent Kresa, then chairman of Northrop, dismissed as "a green eyeshade way." They believed their companies to be consecrated to what they construed as the national interest, and to deserve, in turn, the nation's unconditional support. They believed in McDonnell Douglas. They believed in Rockwell, Hughes, Northrop, Lockheed, General Dynamics, TRW, Litton Industries. They believed in the impossibility of adapting even the most elementary market principles to the manufacturing of aircraft. They believed the very notion of "fixed price," which was the shorthand contractors used to indicate that the government was threatening not to pay for cost overruns, to be antithetical to innovation, anathema to a process that was by its own definition undefined and uncertain.

Since this was an industry in which machine parts were drilled to within two-thousandths or even one-thousandth of an inch, tolerances that did not immediately lend themselves to automation, the people who worked in these plants had never, as they put it, gone robotic. They were the last of the medieval hand workers, and the spaces in which they worked, the huge structures with the immaculate white floors and the big rigs and the overhead cameras and the project banners and the flags of the foreign buyers, became the cathedrals of the Cold War, occasionally visited by but never entirely legible to the uninitiated. "Assembly lines are like living things," I was once told by the manager of assembly operations on the F/A-18 line at Northrop in El Segundo. "A line will gain momentum and build toward a delivery. I can touch it, I can feel it. Here on the line we're a little more blunt and to the point, because this is where the rubber meets the road. If we're going to ship an airplane every two days, we need people to respond to this." *Navy Pilots Are Depending On You*, a banner read in the high shadowy reaches above the F/A-18 line. *Build It As If You Were Going to Fly It*, another read. A toolbox carried this message: *With God & Guts & Guns Our Freedom Was Won!*

This was a world bounded by a diminishing set of coordinates. There were from the beginning a finite number of employers who needed what these people knew how to deliver, and what these people knew how to deliver was only one kind of product. "Our industry's record at defense conversion is unblemished by success," Norman Augustine, then the chairman and CEO of Martin Marietta, told *The Washington Post* in 1993. "Why is it rocket scientists can't sell toothpaste? Because we don't know the market, or how to research, or how to market the product. Other than that, we're in good shape."

Increasingly, the prime aerospace contractors had come to define themselves as "integrators," meaning that a larger and larger proportion of what they delivered, in some cases as much as seventy-five percent, had been supplied by subcontractors. The prime contractors were of course competitive with one another, but there was also an interdependence, a recognition that they had, vis-à-vis their shared principal customer, the federal government, a mutual interest. In this spirit, two or three competing contractors would typically "team" a project, submitting a joint bid, supporting one another during the lobbying phase, and finally dividing the spoils of production.

McDonnell Douglas had been the prime contractor on the F/A-18, an attack aircraft used by both the Navy and the Marine Corps and sold by the Air Force to such foreign users as the Republic of Korea, Malaysia, Australia, Canada, Spain, and Kuwait. McDonnell Douglas, however, teamed the F/A-18 with Northrop, which would every week send, from its El Segundo plant, two partial airplanes, called "shipsets," to the McDonnell Douglas facility in St. Louis. Each Northrop shipset for the F/A-18 included the fuselage and two tails, "stuffed," which is what aircraft people say to indicate that a piece of an airplane comes complete with its working components. McDonnell Douglas would then assemble the shipsets with the wings and other components, and roll the finished F/A-18s off its own line. Northrop and McDonnell Douglas again teamed on a prototype for the YF-23 Advanced Tactical Fighter, but lost the contract to Lockheed, which had teamed its own ATF prototype with Boeing and General Dynamics. Boeing, in turn, teamed its commercial 747 with Northrop, which supplied several 747 shipsets a month, each consisting of the center fuselage and associated sub-assemblies, or stuffing. General Dynamics had the prime contract with the Navy for the A-12 attack jet, but had teamed it with McDonnell Douglas.

The perfect circularity of the enterprise, one in which politicians controlled the letting of government contracts to companies which in turn utilized the contracts to employ potential voters, did not encourage natural selection. When any single element changed in this hermetic and interrelated world, for example a shift in the political climate enabling even one member of Congress to sense a gain in questioning the cost of even one DOD project, the interrelatedness tended to work against adaptation. One tree falls and the food chain fails: on the day in 1991 when Richard B. Cheney, then secretary of defense, finally canceled the Navy's contract with General Dynamics for the

A-12, thousands of McDonnell Douglas jobs got wiped out in St. Louis, where McDonnell Douglas had been teaming the A-12 with General Dynamics.

To protect its headquarters plant in St. Louis, McDonnell Douglas moved some of the production on its own C-17 program from Long Beach to St. Louis. To protect the program itself, the company opened a C-17 plant in Macon, Georgia, what was called in the industry a "double-hitter," situated as it was in both the home state of Senator Sam Nunn, chairman of the Senate Armed Services Committee, and the home district of Rep. J. Roy Rowland, a member of the House Veterans' Affairs Committee. "It was smart business to put a plant in Macon," a former McDonnell Douglas executive told Ralph Vartabedian of *The Los Angeles Times.* "There wouldn't be a C-17 without Nunn's support. There is nothing illegal or immoral about wanting to keep your program funded."

The C-17 was a cargo plane with a capacity for landing, as its supporters frequently mentioned, "on short runways like in Bosnia." It entered development in the mid-1980s. By the time the first plane was delivered in 1993 the number of planes on order from the Air Force had dropped from 210 to 120 and the projected cost of each had risen from $150 million to $380 million. The C-17, even more than most programs, had been plagued by cost overruns and technical problems. There were flaws in the landing gear, a problem with the flaps, trouble meeting range and payload specifications. One test aircraft leaked fuel. Another emerged from a ground strength-certification test with broken wings. Once off the ground, the plane showed a distressing readiness to pitch up its nose and go into a stall.

On June 14, 1993, the day the Air Force accepted delivery of its first C-17 Globemaster III, the plane was more than a year behind schedule, already $1.4 billion over budget, and not yet within sight of a final design determination. Considerable show attended this delivery. Many points were made. The ceremony took place at Charleston Air Force Base in South Carolina, the home state of Senator Strom Thurmond, then the ranking minority member of the Senate Armed Services Committee, as well as of Representatives Floyd Spence, John M. Spratt, Jr., and Arthur Ravenal, Jr., all members of the House Armed Services Committee. Some thirty-five hundred officials turned out. The actual aircraft, which was being delivered with 125 "waivers and deviations" from contract specifications and had been flown east with a load of ballast positioned to keep the nose from pitching up, was piloted on its delivery leg by General Merrill McPeak, the Air Force chief of staff. "We had it loaded with Army equipment . . . a couple of Humvees, twenty or thirty soldiers painted up for battle," General McPeak reported a few days later at a Pentagon briefing. "And I would just say that it's a fine airplane, wonderful capability when we get it fielded, it will make a big difference to us in terms of the global mobility requirement we have, and so I just think, you know, it's a home run."

At the time General McPeak pronounced the plane a home run, 8,700 of the remaining employees at McDonnell Douglas's Long Beach plant were working on the

C-17. What those 8,700 employees would be doing the month or the year after that remained, at that time, an open question, since even as the Air Force was demonstrating support of its own program, discussions had begun about how best to dispose of it. There were a number of options under consideration. One was to transfer program management from McDonnell Douglas to Boeing. Another was to further reduce the number of C-17s on order from 120 to as few as 25. The last-ditch option, the A-12 solution, was to just pull the plug. The Long Beach plant was the plant on the Lakewood city line, the plant with the American flag whipping in the wind and the forward-slanted logo and the boarded-up motel with the marquee that still read "Welcome Douglas Happy Hour 4–7." This was what people in Lakewood were talking about when they talked about the Spur Posse.

6

O F the eighty-nine members of the Lakewood
High School Class of 1989 who had responded, a
year after graduation, to a school district ques-
tionnaire asking what they were doing, seventy-one said
that they were attending college full or part time. Forty-
two of those were enrolled at Long Beach Community
College. Five were at community colleges in the neighboring communities of Cerritos and Cypress. Twelve were
at various nearby California State University campuses:
Fullerton, Long Beach, San Diego, Pomona. Two had been
admitted to the University of California system, one to
Irvine and one to Santa Barbara. One was at U.S.C. Nine
were at unspecified other campuses. During the 1990–91
school year, 234 Lakewood High students were enrolled
in the district's magnet program in aerospace technology,
which channeled into Long Beach Community College
and McDonnell Douglas. Lakewood High's SAT scores
for that year averaged 362 verbal and 440 math, a total of
ninety-five points below the state average.

This was not a community that pushed its children
hard, or launched them into the far world. Males were
encouraged to continue, after graduation and indeed into

adulthood, playing ball (many kinds of ball, all kinds of ball) in the parks and on the schoolgrounds where they had grown up. Females were encouraged to participate in specific sports of their own, as well as to support the team activities of the ball players. Virtually everyone to whom I spoke in the spring of 1993 mentioned the city's superior sports program. "It's been a very clean community," I was told by John Todd, who had been instrumental in the city's 1954 incorporation and had served as city attorney ever since. "The people that made it up were sound American citizens. We were oriented to our schools and churches and other local activities. We have a tremendous park and recreation program here in Lakewood. And it tended to keep people here." Another longtime resident, whose oldest son worked for McDonnell Douglas and whose other grown children were all in school nearby, echoed this: "It's just a mass recreation program to keep them all busy."

People in Lakewood often mentioned to me how much there was going on in the area. There were the batting cages. There was bowling. There were many movies around. There was, nearby in Downey, the campaign to preserve the nation's last operating original McDonald's, a relic of 1953 at the corner of Lakewood Boulevard and Florence Avenue. "If they're going to tear this down, they might as well tell Clinton please take your business to Taco Bell," one observer told the *Press-Telegram.* And there was, always, the mall, Lakewood Center, the actual and figurative center of town. During the days I spent in Lakewood I had occasion to visit the mall now and then, and each time I found it moderately busy, the fact that its sales figures had decreased every quarter since 1990 notwithstanding. There was a reflecting pool, a carousel, a Burger King, a McDonald's, if not an original McDonald's. There was a booth offering free information on prescriptions. There was another displaying photographs of houses for sale. I said to a woman leafing through the listings that I had not before seen houses for sale in a mall. "H.U.D. and V.A. repos," she said.

One day at the mall I walked over to the freestanding Bullock's, which, because it was about to close its doors for good, was in the process of selling everything in the store at thirty-five percent off the ticket price. There were women systematically defoliating the racks in the men's-wear department, women dropping discards and hangers in tangles on the floor, women apparently undiscouraged by the scrawled sign warning that register lines were "currently in excess of 3+ hours long," women who had already staked out positions for the wait, women curled with their children on the floor, women who had bulwarked their positions with forts of quilts, comforters, bedspreads, mattress pads, Cuisinarts, coffee makers, sandwich grills, Juice Tigers, and Heart Wafflers. These were the women and the daughters and granddaughters of the women who had seen the hundred-foot pylon in 1950 and decided that this was the place to start. The clerks and security personnel monitoring the register lines were men. These were the men and the sons and grandsons of the men who used to get what seemed like half the A-4 line out to watch Little League.

7

"WE want great cities, large factories, and mines worked cheaply, in this California of ours!" That was Henry George, in "What the Railroad Will Bring Us," rhetorically setting forth what was in 1868 popular local sentiment. Then he proceeded to count the cost:

> Would we esteem ourselves gainers if New York, ruled and robbed by thieves, loafers and brothel-keepers; nursing a race of savages fiercer and meaner than any who ever shrieked a war-whoop on the plains; could be set down on our bay tomorrow? Would we be gainers, if the cotton-mills of Massachusetts, with their thousands of little children who, official papers tell us, are being literally worked to death, could be transported to the banks of the American; or the file and pin factories of England, where young girls are treated worse than even slaves on southern plantations, be reared as if by magic at Antioch? Or if among our mountains we could by wishing have the miners, men, women and children, who

work the iron and coal mines of Belgium and France, where the condition of production is that the laborer shall have meat but once a week—would we wish them here?

Can we have one thing without the other?

In those towns off the San Diego Freeway that had seemed when times were good to answer Henry George's question in the affirmative, 1993 was a sullen spring. In April, about the time the Lakewood Center Bullock's was selling the last of its Heart Wafflers, the ten-year-old girl who said that she had been assaulted by a Spur Posse member gave her first press conference, in Gloria Allred's office. Her mother had been seen, on *Donahue, The Home Show,* and *20/20,* but the child, by that time eleven, had not. "I have been upset because I wanted to be on TV," she said at her press conference. "To show how I feel. I wanted to say it for myself." Also in April, Spur Posse members approached various talent agencies, trying to sell their story for a TV movie. An I.C.M. agent asked these Spurs if they were not concerned about how they might be presented. Their concern, they told him, was how much money they would make. I.C.M. declined to represent the Spurs, as did, it was later reported, C.A.A., United Talent Agency, and William Morris.

It was April, too, at the Douglas plant on the Lakewood city line, when Teamsters Local 692 went on strike, over the issue of whether or not Douglas could contract out work previously done by union members. "They can't do that to people after twenty-seven years," the wife of one driver, for whom the new contract would mean a cut from $80,000 to $35,000 a year, told the *Press-Telegram.* "It's just not right." It was in April, again, that Finnair disclosed discussions about a switch from its mostly Douglas fleet to buying Boeing. It was in May that Continental, just out of bankruptcy reorganization, ordered ninety-two new planes, with options for ninety-eight more, all from Boeing.

In a town where it was possible to hear, unprompted, a spirited defense of the DC-10 ("Very quiet plane," John Todd told me, "nice flying plane, compared to those Boeings and those other airplanes it makes about half as much noise"), the involvement with Douglas went deeper than mere economic dependence. People in Lakewood had defined their lives as Douglas. I had lunch one day with a 1966 graduate of Lakewood High who had later spent time in the Peace Corps. It seemed that somewhere in the heart of Africa, he had hopped a ride on a DC-3. The DC-3 had a plate indicating that it had come off the Long Beach line, and he had thought, There it is, I've come as far as I can go and it's still Douglas. "It's a town on the plantation model," he said to me at lunch. "Douglas being the big house."

"They're history," an aircraft industry executive said that spring to *The Washington Post.* "I see a company going out of business, barring some miracle," Don E. Newquist, chairman of the International Trade Commission, said at a hearing on commercial aerospace competitiveness. Each was talking about Douglas, and by extension about the

plant on the Lakewood city line, the plant with the flag
and the forward-slanted logo and the MD-11s parked
like cars and the motel with the marquee that still read
"Welcome Douglas Happy Hour 4–7." "It's like a lifetime
thing," one Lakewood High graduate said on *Jane Whitney,* trying to explain the Spur Posse and what held its
members together. "We're all going to be friends for life,
you know."

It was 1997 when Douglas was finally melted into
Boeing, and the forward-slanted letters reading
MCDONNELL DOUGLAS vanished from what was
now the Boeing plant on the Lakewood city line.

It was 1999 when Boeing shut down Douglas's
MD-90 program.

It was 2000 when Boeing shut down Douglas's
MD-80 program, 2001 when Boeing shut down Douglas's MD-11 program.

It was 2000 when Boeing began talking about its plan
to convert two hundred and thirty acres of what had been
the Douglas plant into non-aircraft use, in fact a business
park, "PacifiCenter," with its own condominium housing
and the dream of attracting, with what inducements
became increasingly unclear as the economy waned, such
firms as Intel and Sun Microsystems.

It was 2002 when Boeing obtained an order from the
Pentagon for sixty additional C-17s, another temporary
stay of execution for what had been the Douglas program,

which had been scheduled for closure in 2004. "It's a great day," the manager on the program told employees on the day he announced the order. "This is going to keep you employed through 2008, so rest tonight and start on sixty more tomorrow."

It was also 2002 when the first stage of a multi-billion-dollar public works project called the "Alameda Corridor" was completed, a $2.4 billion twenty-mile express railway meant to speed freight containers from the ports of Long Beach and Los Angeles to inland distribution points. This "Alameda Corridor" had been for some years a kind of model civic endeavor, one of those political mechanisms designed to reward old friends and make new ones. During the period when the Alameda Corridor was still only an idea, but an idea moving inexorably toward a start date, its supporters frequently framed it as the way to bring a "new economy" to the twenty-six "Gateway Cities" involved, all of which had been dependent on aerospace and one of which was Lakewood. This "new economy" was to be built on "international trade," an entirely theoretical replacement for the gold-standard money tree, the federal government, that had created these communities. Many seminars on "global logistics" were held. Many warehouses were built. The first stage of the Alameda Corridor was near completion before people started wondering what exactly these warehouses were to bring them; started wondering, for example, whether eight-dollars-an-hour forklift operators, hired in the interests of a "flexible" work force only on those days when the warehouse was receiving or dispatching freight, could ever become the "good citizens" of whom Mark Taper had spoken in 1969, the "enthusiastic owners of property," the "owners of a piece of their country—a stake in the land." *California likes to be fooled,* as Cedarquist, the owner in *The Octopus* of the failed San Francisco iron works, told Presley at the Bohemian Club.

In 1970 I was working for *Life,* and went up to eastern Oregon to do a piece on the government's storage of VX and GB nerve gas on twenty thousand acres near Hermiston, a farm town in Umatilla County, population then 5,300. It seemed that many citizens wanted the nerve gas, or, in the preferred term, "the defense material," the storage of which provided 717 civilian jobs and brought money into town. It seemed that other citizens, some of whom lived not in Hermiston but across the mountains in Portland and Salem, making them members of what was referred to in Hermiston as "the academic community and Other Mothers for Peace or whatever," saw the presence in Oregon of VX and GB as a hazard. The story was routine enough, and I had pretty much wrapped it up (seen the mayor, seen the city manager, seen the anti-gas district attorney in Pendleton, seen the colonel in charge of the depot and seen the rabbits they left in the bunkers to test for leaks) before I realized that the situation had for me an actual resonance: since well before Elizabeth Scott was born, members of my family had been moving through places in the same spirit of care-less self-interest and optimism that now seemed to be powering this argument in Hermiston. Such was the power of the story on which I had grown up that this thought came to me as a kind of revelation: the settlement of the west, however inevitable, had not uniformly tended to the greater good, nor had it on every level benefitted even those who reaped its most obvious rewards.

One afternoon in September of 2002 I drove the length of the Alameda Corridor, north from the port through what had been the industrial heart of Southern California: Carson, Compton, Watts. Lynwood, South Gate. Huntington Park. Vernon. It was a few weeks before that fall's dockworkers' strike shut down Pacific trade, and I saw that afternoon no trains, no containers, only this new rail line meant to carry the freight and these new warehouses meant to house the freight, many of them bear-ing for-lease signs. On the first hill north of Signal Hill there was what appeared to be a new subdivision, with a sign, "Vista Industria." Past the sign that read Vista Indus-tria there were only more warehouses, miles of warehouses, miles of empty intersections, one Gateway City after another, each indistinguishable from the last. Only when the Arco Towers began emerging from the distant haze over downtown Los Angeles did I notice a sign on a ware-house that seemed to suggest actual current usage. *165,000 Square Feet of T-Shirt Madness,* this sign read.

S ave the Aero—See "Tadpole." This was the sign on the
Aero Theatre on Montana Avenue in Santa Monica in
September of 2002. The Aero Theatre was built in 1939
by Donald Douglas, as recreation for his workers when
Douglas Aircraft was Santa Monica's biggest employer.
During the ten years when I was living not far from the
Aero, 1978 to 1988, I never saw anyone actually enter or
leave the theatre. Douglas built Santa Monica and then
left it, and the streets running south of what had been the
first Douglas plant were now lined with body shops, mini-
marts, Pentecostal churches and walk-in dentists. Still,
Santa Monica had its ocean, its beaches, its climate, its sun
and its fog and its climbing roses. The Gateway Cities
will have only their warehouses.

Part Three

I

"What had it all been about: all the manqué promises, the failures of love and faith and honor; Martha buried out there by the levee in a $250 dress from Magnin's with river silt in the seams; Sarah in Bryn Mawr, Pennsylvania; her father, who had not much cared, the easy loser (*He never could have been,* her mother had said and still loved him); her mother sitting alone this afternoon in the big house upriver writing out invitations for the Admission Day Fiesta and watching *Dick Clark's American Bandstand* because the Dodgers were rained out; Everett down there on the dock with his father's .38. She, her mother, Everett, Martha, the whole family gallery: they carried the same blood, come down through twelve generations of circuit riders, county sheriffs, Indian fighters, country lawyers, Bible readers, one obscure United States senator from a frontier state a long time ago; two hundred years of clearings in Virginia and Kentucky and Tennessee and then the break, the void into which they gave their rosewood chests, their silver brushes; the cutting clean which was to have redeemed them all. They had been a particular kind of people, their particular virtues called up by a particular situation, their particular flaws waiting there through all those years, unperceived, unsuspected, glimpsed only cloudily by one or two in each generation, by a wife whose bewildered eyes wanted to look not upon Eldorado but upon her mother's dogwood, by a blue-eyed boy who was at sixteen the best shot in the county and who when there was nothing left to shoot rode out one day and shot his brother, an accident. It had been above all a history of accidents: of moving on and of accidents. What is it you want, she had asked Everett tonight. It was a question she might have asked them all."

THAT passage is from the last few pages of a novel, *Run River*, published in 1963. The author of the novel was me. The protagonist, the "she" of the passage, is Lily McClellan, born Lily Knight, the wife of a hop grower on the Sacramento River. As the novel opens, Lily's husband, Everett McClellan, has just shot and killed the man with whom both Lily and his sister Martha have had affairs. This story, the "plot" of the novel, was imagined, but the impulse that initially led me to imagine this story and not another was real: I was a year or two out of Berkeley, working for *Vogue* in New York, and experiencing a yearning for California so raw that night after night, on copy paper filched from my office and the Olivetti Lettera 22 I had bought in high school with the money I made stringing for *The Sacramento Union* ("Big mistake buying Italian," my father had advised, "as you'll discover the first time you need a part replaced"), I sat on one of my apartment's two chairs and set the Olivetti on the other and wrote myself a California river.

The "stuff" of the novel, then, was the landscape and weather of the Sacramento Valley, the way the rivers crested and the way the tule fogs obscured the levees and the way the fallen camellias turned the sidewalks brown and slick during the Christmas rains. The stuff, too, was in the way those rains and those rivers had figured in the stories I had been told my entire life, stories predicated on the childhood memories of relatives (Kilgores and Reeses, Jerretts and Farnsworths, Magees and Cornwalls) who were by then long dead themselves, fragments of local oral history preserved by daughters and granddaughters on legal pads and the backs of envelopes:

That winter was a very wet winter, raining night and day for weeks. It was always called the winter of the Flood as the levee broke on the east side of Sacramento and the city was a lake of water, boats running up and down the streets and small houses floating around like dry goods boxes. This was in 1861 and 1862.

During the flood it was impossible to get any provisions out of Sacramento, only by boat, so three of our neighbors who were out of tobacco, Wm. Scholefield, Myron Smith and a man by the name of Sidell, built a boat out of rough boards and launched it in the creek on Scholefield's place and went to Sacramento by water, two rowing and one bailing the water out. They made the round trip and brought home their tobacco and some provisions.

The downpour continued and the river swelled until the banks overflowed. The families were soon engulfed by the water. They gathered as much of their belongings as were salvageable and moved by rowboat to a two-story house on the Grape Vine Ranch, about one-half mile away.

The importance of recording these memories was unquestioned: the flood and the levees and the two-story house on the Grape Vine Ranch had become, like the potato masher that crossed the plains, like the books that did not get jettisoned on the Umpqua River, evidence of family endurance, proof of our worth, indistinguishable from the crossing story itself.

During this time Elizabeth became critically ill. It was typhoid. Allen and one of the Kilgore cousins rowed through the storm to Sacramento for necessary supplies. The current of the rampant river flood raged about them and it took two days and nights to reach the settlement city. The morning following Allen's return, Elizabeth died. Allen built a coffin for Elizabeth and the women dressed her in a garment of coarse white cotton. The coffin was rowed to hilly ground where there were already other graves. The ground was so full of water that the grave was like a well. Here Elizabeth was buried as there was no other place available.

"Two hundred years of clearings in Virginia and Kentucky and Tennessee and then the break, the void into which they gave their rosewood chests, their silver brushes, the cutting clean which was to have redeemed them all." This was the crossing story as origin myth, the official history as I had learned it. Although certain other lines in that passage from *Run River* suggest that I was beginning to entertain some doubt ("what had it all been about," "a history of accidents: of moving on and of accidents"), the passage now raises questions that did not at the time occur to me. From what exactly was "the break" or "the void" or "the cutting clean" to have redeemed them? From their Scotch-Irish genes? From the idealization that had alchemized the luckless of Wales and Scotland and Ireland into classless western yeomen? From the confusions that led both Jack London and *The Valley of the Moon*'s Saxon Brown to claim the special rights they believed due them as "old American stock"? Or were they to have been redeemed from the break itself, the "cutting clean," "the void"? And the related question: for *what* were they to have been redeemed? To make of their lives, as Nancy Hardin Cornwall was said to have made of hers,

"one ceaseless round of activity"? To "live up to our heritage," as I put it in my eighth-grade graduation speech,
and "go on to better and greater things for California"?
What exactly was our heritage? *Remember,* as Virginia
Reed wrote to her cousin, *never take no cutoffs and hurry
along as fast as you can.*

M uch in *Run River,* as I believed when I was writing
it and as I read it now, some four decades later, has
to do with the ways California was or is "changing," the
detailing of which permeates the novel with a tenacious
(and, as I see it now, pernicious) mood of nostalgia. The
current action (much of the novel is past action) takes
place in August 1959. Everett McClellan's sister Martha
has been dead more than ten years, drowned when she
took a boat onto the river in flood stage. On the March
morning after Martha's death, as Everett and the ranch
foreman dig the grave by the levee in which they will bury
her, Lily concentrates on the river, on where and when the
levee will go, on the "file of information, gathered and
classified every year there was high water. . . . At what
point had they opened the Colusa Weir. How many gates
were open at the Sacramento Weir. When would the
Bypass reach capacity. What was the flood stage at
Wilkins Slough. At Rough and Ready Bend. Fremont
Weir. Rio Vista."

As presented, Martha McClellan's burial on the ranch,
with the river still rising and talk confined to speculation

about whether the Army Engineers will dynamite an upstream levee, would seem to represent an idea of traditional, or "old," California. We are told that Martha herself, as a child, invented a game called "Donner Party," in which she herself starred as Tamsen Donner, and hung on the walls of her room "neither Degas ballet dancers nor scenes from *Alice in Wonderland* but a framed deed signed by John Sutter in 1847, a matted list of the provisions carried on an obscure crossing in 1852, a detailed relief map of the Humboldt Sink, and a large lithograph of Donner Pass on which Martha had printed, in two neat columns, the names of the casualties and survivors of the Donner-Reed crossing." To a similar point, Martha is buried in the sea chest in which her mother, long dead, had kept her linens, along with "ends of lace, a box of jet beading from a dress, and the ivory fan carried by Martha's great-great-grandmother Currier at Governor Leland Stanford's Inaugural Ball in 1862." To lay in the grave, Everett has torn down "whole branches" of camellias, which are presented in the novel as having, since they were planted locally in memory of the pioneers, a totemic significance. If the grave washes out, which it surely will if the river continues rising, Martha (and the totemic camellias) will be "free again in the water," at one with the river, a prospect that seems to deter, as "true" Californians, neither her brother nor her sister-in-law.

The year Martha dies is 1949. By 1959, as presented in *Run River,* this "true" California has been largely obliterated. The pear orchards on which Lily herself grew up are being relentlessly uprooted: her mother is selling off the acreage for development as fast as the bank will allow her to subordinate it. The ranches immediately upriver and downriver from the McClellan ranch are already subdivisions, Rancho Del Rio No. 1 and Rancho Del Rio No. 3. This is unsettling to Everett but not so to his and Lily's son, Knight. "They're just biding their time," Knight says. "Waiting it out for Rancho Del Rio No. 2." Knight is about to go east to college, to Princeton, a "new" kind of choice (the "traditional" choice would have been Berkeley or Stanford) and so, again, unsettling. Knight is full of himself, and lectures his mother, who has asked him, since he is driving to Berkeley, to pick up some new paperback books on Telegraph Avenue. From Knight's point of view:

> She did not seem to realize that there were now paperback bookstores in Sacramento. She and his father would never seem to get it through their heads that things were changing in Sacramento, that Aerojet General and Douglas Aircraft and even the State College were bringing in a whole new class of people, people who had lived back East, people who read things. She and his father were going to be pretty surprised if and when they ever woke up to the fact that nobody in Sacramento any more had even heard of the McClellans. Or the Knights. Not that he thought they ever would wake up. They'd just go right along dedicating their grubby goddamn camellia trees

in Capitol Park to the memory of their grubby goddamn pioneers.

There are other signs of change, which, in the construct of the novel, is understood to mean decline. There is Everett's older sister, Sarah, who lives outside Philadelphia, another "new" kind of choice, with her third husband: again, a new kind of choice. Sarah has stopped by the ranch on her way to Maui (still another new choice, since the traditional Hawaiian destination would be Honolulu, on the *Lurline*), apologized to her husband for the Valley heat ("true" children of the Valley are made uneasy by summer temperatures that do not reach three digits), and made it clear to Everett that she tolerates his wish to keep as ranches rather than subdivide their joint inheritance, seven thousand acres on the Sacramento and Cosumnes Rivers, only as a provisional indulgence. "Surely we've had offers," Sarah suggests to Everett. Everett allows that interest has been expressed in the ranch on the Cosumnes. "I don't *care* so much about the Cosumnes," Sarah says. "The Cosumnes at least brings in a little cash."

There is also the man Everett will eventually shoot, Ryder Channing. Ryder Channing is the only character in the novel not "from" California, in other words one of the "new people." He first meets Martha in 1944, when he is stationed at Mather Field in Sacramento, and his appearances on the ranch to see her, which continue, inexplicably to Everett, after the war has ended and this person not from California should have gone home to wherever he came from, are presented as troubling elements. He has no intention of leaving, he tells Everett, because California is where the future is being made:

Starting now. Channing had the hunch they were in on the ground floor of the biggest boom this country had ever seen. Talk about your gold rush. And he wasn't the only one who believed in Northern California. Just one example, the Keller Brothers believed in Northern California to the tune of five million berries.

"The Keller Brothers," Everett said. "I don't believe I know them."

The Keller Brothers, Channing explained patiently, were developers. Los Angeles developers who believed in Northern California, in the Valley specifically, to the tune of five million smackeroos. Which they were putting into the Natomas District.

"I never heard of any Kellers in the Natomas," Everett said.

With what appeared to be infinite restraint, Channing inspected and crumpled three empty cigarette packages before answering. "They aren't in the Natomas right now. They want to develop the Natomas."

"Who's putting up the money? How can they raise five million dollars on land they haven't got?"

"Those sweethearts could raise five million dollars with a plot plan on the back of a goddamn napkin. Anyway," Channing added, apparently abandoning his effort to justify the Kellers' ways to Everett, "that's just one example. The point is we're sitting right here on the ground floor with the button pushed go."

Ryder, who because he has no California heritage is incapable of betraying it, not only sees the future but seizes it: he abandons Martha in 1948 to marry the daughter of a recently rich developer. ("Construction money, Everett believed. Wartime. It was all mixed up in his mind with Henry Kaiser.") Martha, about whom there have been previous suggestions of histrionic instability (at parties the year she was sixteen "it had been impossible not to notice her, as it might have been impossible not to notice someone running a high fever, or wearing a cellophane dress"), spends the winter between Ryder's marriage and her own death trying in vain to embrace this New California from which Ryder had come and to which she has now lost him: "She went everywhere, met everyone. She met builders, promoters, people looking for factory sites and talking about a deep-water channel and lobbying for federal dams; people neither Everett nor Lily would have known existed had she not told them. She went to large parties at new country clubs, went to small parties at new apartment houses, and went, almost every afternoon, to inspect subdivisions opened by one or another of the boys she knew who were going into the real estate business."

This is a not inaccurate characterization of the way Sacramento, or for that matter California itself, felt to a child growing up during the postwar boom years, the late 1940s and early 1950s; sometimes, say when I hear about what the Alameda Corridor will bring us, I still catch the echo of those years. It was true that it was suddenly possible, as if overnight, to buy paperback books at Levinson's bookstore downtown. It was true that it was suddenly possible, as if overnight, to see foreign movies—*Open City, The Bicycle Thief,* a lachrymose Swedish young-love picture called *One Summer of Happiness*—at the Guild Theater in Oak Park, although the only member of my family to regularly see them was a half-deaf great-aunt for whom subtitles offered the novel possibility of actually following the action onscreen. It was true that the habits and customs of "old Sacramento" (the school-vacation jobs on the ranches and at the canneries, the swimming in the rivers and wading in the ditches, the dutiful study of the agricultural exhibits at the California State Fair) were giving way to a more urban, or suburban, life, in which children swam in clear water in backyard pools lined with gunite and bought Italian typewriters and ate pears bought in supermarkets rather than dropped off in lugs by the relatives who grew them.

All this was true, and yet there was in *Run River* something that was not true, a warp, a persistent suggestion that these changes brought about by World War Two had in some way been resisted by "true" Californians. Had not any such resistance been confined to the retrospect? Were not "changes" and "boom years" what the California experience had been about since the first American settlement? Were we not still willing to traffic our own history to get what the railroad could bring us?

Take for example this business of laying the iconic camellias in Martha's grave: in point of fact the whole notion of planting camellias for the pioneers—there was in the park across from the state capitol building in Sacramento a "Camellia Grove" set aside for this purpose—had originated with my father's stepmother, Genevieve Didion, who was for many years the president of the Sacramento City Board of Education and was said by the rest of the family, not entirely approvingly, to be "political." All association of camellias with pioneers, in other words, derived from the same spirit of civic boosterism that would later turn Front Street, along the river, into the entirely ersatz "redevelopment" known as "Old Sacramento," twenty-eight riverfront acres of shops selling trinkets and souvenirs and popcorn. "The pioneers," in other words, had become a promotional tool, Sacramento's own unique selling proposition, a way of attracting tourists, conventions, a new kind of cash that did not depend on crops: one more version of the weakness for the speculative venture that Charles Nordhoff had noted in 1874.

"The pool kills me," Everett McClellan's sister Sarah says, in *Run River,* when she visits the ranch on which he and Lily live. "It looks like Pickfair."

The year Sarah says this is 1959. Although swimming pools were fairly general throughout California by

1959, this pool on the ranch represents, as presented, Everett's first concession to the postwar mood, and so cues the reader to yet another sign of decline. This did not exactly reflect any attitude toward pools with which I was familiar.

In 1948, when my mother and father and brother and I were living on some acreage outside Sacramento on which my father had built a house until the time seemed right to subdivide the property, my brother and I wanted a pool. We could have a pool, my father said, but only if we ourselves dug it. Every morning all that hot summer my brother, Jim, who was eight, took a shovel out to the middle of the field in front of the house and chipped in vain at the hardpan that underlay the inch or two of topsoil.

Five years older than Jim, doubtful that either he or I could dig a twenty-by-forty-foot hole eight feet deep, equally doubtful that our father—were such a hole to miraculously materialize—had any intention of following through (as I saw it, he might string a hose out there and turn on the tap, but no gunite, no filter, no tile coping), I declined to dig. Instead I spent the summer reading the plays of Eugene O'Neill and dreamed of escaping to Bennington, where I would prepare myself for a New York life in the theater by sitting in a tree in a leotard and listening to Francis Fergusson explain the difference between drama and melodrama. This was the year, 1948, when, already plotting my departure, I delivered the eighth-grade graduation speech on "Our California Heritage." This was also the year, 1948, when the Sacramento

City Parks Department awarded, as prizes in its annual Easter egg hunt, what *The Sacramento Bee* described as "live bunnies named after pioneers," a teaching tool, it occurs to me now, that had "Genevieve Didion" written all over it. Ten years later I did have a New York life, although not in the theater, and I was writing the novel that would put such a protective distance between me and the place I came from.

2

THIS question of "changes," involving as it does some reflexive suggestion of a birthright squandered, a paradise lost, is a vexed issue. I was many times told as a child that the grass in the Sacramento Valley had at the time the American settlers arrived in the 1840s grown so high that it could be tied over a saddle, the point being that it did no more. California, in this telling, had even then been "spoiled." The logical extension of this thought, that we were the people who had spoiled it, remained unexplored. Nor would it be explored in *Run River,* the inchoate intent of which was to return me to a California I wished had been there to keep me. *"Everything changes, everything changed,"* one passage, obviously acutely felt at the time I wrote it, begins. *"Summer evenings driving downriver to auctions, past the green hops in leaf, blackbirds flying up from the brush in the dry twilight air, red Christmas-tree balls glittering in the firelight, a rush of autumn Sundays, all gone, when you drove through the rain to visit the great-aunts."* The "change," the "all gone" part, is seen in *Run River* to have come only with the postwar boom years, the prosperous years when California "as it was" got bulldozed out of existence either for better (as

Ben Weingart and Louis Boyar and Mark Taper saw it when they conceived Lakewood) or (as I then wished to see it) for worse.

Californians of more programmatic mind for many years presented these postwar changes as positive, the very genius of the place: it was conventional to mention the freeway system, the aerospace industry, the University of California Master Plan, Silicon Valley, the massive rearrangement of the water that got funded when Pat Brown was governor, the entire famous package, the celebrated promise that California was committed to creating and educating an apparently infinitely expandable middle class. The more recent programmatic attitude was to construe the same changes as negative, false promises: the freeways had encouraged sprawl, the aerospace industry had gone away, the University of California had lost faculty and classrooms to budget cuts, Silicon Valley had put housing beyond the means of non-tech California, and most of the state was still short water.

In a book of readings for students in freshman composition classes at California colleges, the editors and contributors speak of "the threats to the California dream," of the need to keep "the California dream in sight," of "the fashionable new mythology emerging nationwide in which California is being recast as a nightmare rather than a dream," and of which O. J. Simpson—O. J. Simpson as "the self-invented celebrity who climbed from poverty to the summit of fame and fortune" or O. J. Simpson in the white Bronco—"better reflects the truth about the California dream." In either case, genius of the place or its dystopian blight, the postwar changes that transformed California were understood to have been brought about by what was popularly seen as an unprecedented influx of population, what Pat Brown, in a 1962 issue of *Look,* called "the greatest mass migration in the history of the world" and George B. Leonard, in the same issue of *Look,* called "the migrating millions who vote with their wheels for California." During World War Two and the immediate postwar years, 1940 to 1950, the population of California did in fact increase 53 percent. During the next ten years, 1950 to 1960, the population of California did in fact increase 49 percent.

Yet such growth was in no way unprecedented. Nor, in a state that had seen its population increase in the first ten years of statehood by 245 percent, was it even remarkable. The decade between 1860 and 1870 brought a population increase to California of 47 percent, the decade that followed an increase of 54 percent. The years between 1900 and 1910 brought another 60 percent. Those were the years during which Faulkner's Ira Ewing, in "Golden Land," would have fled Nebraska on the night train to end up twenty-five years later sleepless in Beverly Hills. The years between 1910 and 1920 brought 44 percent. Those were the years when it came to the attention of Saxon Brown and Billy Roberts in *The Valley of the Moon* that "it looks like the free-born American ain't got no room left in his own land"—two babes convinced that they had been deprived of their Eden by industrialization, by immigration, by whatever it was that they could not name. The ten years that followed, between 1920 and 1930, when

only shallowly settled arrivals were to find themselves further marginalized by the onset of the Depression, brought
66 percent. There had been, then, from the beginning,
these obliterating increases, rates of growth that systematically erased freshly laid traces of custom and community,
and it was from such erasures that many California confusions would derive.

There used to be on the main street through Gilroy, a
farm town in Santa Clara County that billed itself as
"The Garlic Capital of the World," a two- or three-story
hotel, the Milias, where the dining room off the lobby had
a black-and-white tiled floor and fans and potted palm
trees and, in the opinion of my father, short ribs so succu-
lent that they were worth a stop on any drive between
Sacramento and the Monterey Peninsula. I remember
sitting with him in the comparative cool of the Milias
dining room (any claim of "cool" was at that time comparative, air conditioning not yet having taken widespread
hold in Santa Clara County), eating short ribs and the
cherries from his old-fashioned bourbon cocktail, the sin-
gular musky smell of garlic being grown and picked and
processed permeating even the heavy linen napkins.

I am unsure at what point the Milias Hotel vanished
(probably about the time Santa Clara County started
being called Silicon Valley), but it did, and the "farm
town" vanished too, Gilroy having reinvented itself as a
sprawl of commuter subdivisions for San Jose and the tech
industry. In the summer of 2001, a local resident named

Michael Bonfante opened a ninety-million-dollar theme park in Gilroy, "Bonfante Gardens," the attractions of which were designed to suggest the agricultural: stage shows with singing tomatoes, rides offering the possibility of being spun in a giant garlic bulb or swung from a thirty-nine-foot-high mushroom. The intention behind Bonfante Gardens, according to its creator, was "to show how the county was in the 1950s and 1960s." The owner of a neighboring property was interviewed by *The New York Times* on the subject of Bonfante Gardens. "If it gets to be Disneyland, I am going to hate it," she said. "Right now it is pretty and beautiful. But who knows? Someone who has been here as long as I have has mixed feelings."

This interviewee, according to the *Times,* had been a resident of Gilroy, in other words "been here," for fifteen years. If fifteen years seems somewhat short of the long-time settlement suggested by "someone who has been here as long as I have," consider this: when my brother and I applied to change the zoning from agricultural to residential on a ranch we owned east of Sacramento, one of the most active opponents to the change, a man who spoke passionately to the folly of so altering the nature of the area, had moved to California only six months before, which suggested that he was living on a street that existed only because somebody else had developed a ranch. Discussion of how California has "changed," then, tends locally to define the more ideal California as that which existed at whatever past point the speaker first saw it: Gilroy as it was in the 1960s and Gilroy as it was fifteen years ago and Gilroy as it was when my father and I ate short ribs at the Milias Hotel are three pictures with virtually no overlap, a hologram that dematerializes as I drive through it.

Victor Davis Hanson is a professor of classics on the Fresno campus of California State University, a contributor of occasional opinion pieces to *The New York Times* and *The Wall Street Journal,* and the author of a number of books, including *The Land Was Everything: Letters from an American Farmer,* an impassioned polemic modeled on and informed by J. Hector St. John de Crèvecoeur's 1782 *Letters from an American Farmer.* Hanson has in fact for most of his life thought of himself as a farmer, either active or failed (he rejects the word "grower," more common in California, as "a term of self-approbation, used by those in California who often do not themselves grow anything"), with his brother and cousins a cultivator of grapevines and fruit trees on the same San Joaquin Valley land, fewer than two hundred acres, that their great-great-grandfather homesteaded in the 1870s. He sees himself as heir to the freeholding yeomen farmers who, in Crèvecoeur's and his own view, "created the American republican spirit." He tells us that his children are the sixth consecutive generation to live in the same house. The single photograph I have seen of him shows a man in his forties, wearing khakis and a T-shirt, his features and general stance so characteristic of the Central Valley (a good deal of sun exposure goes into this look, and a certain wary defiance) that the photograph could seem indistinguishable from snapshots of my father and cousins.

There is much in *The Land Was Everything* that catches exactly this Valley note. There is the smell of insecticides, fungicides, the toxic mists that constitute the smell of the place. ("What they're trying to do is generate a new fear of the word 'carcinogen,'" the corporate counsel for the J. G. Boswell Company, which operates fifty thousand acres in the Tulare Basin, famously said in response to certain restrictions placed during the mid-1980s on the use of toxic chemicals. "Chemicals are absolutely necessary for everyday life.") There is the sense of walking the ditches in an orchard, losing oneself among the propped limbs of the overburdened fruit trees. There is the visceral pleasure of cold Sierra water as it comes from the flume. There is the monosyllabic speech pattern, the directness to the point of rudeness, the abrupt way of launching and ending telephone calls with no niceties, no identification, no salutation, no goodbye, just a hangup. I never once heard my father's father, the grandfather who remained "Mr. Didion" to me, identify himself on the telephone. My mother frequently hung up without saying goodbye, sometimes in midsentence. "I do not think I shall leave the San Joaquin Valley of California," Hanson writes. "Courage, a friend tells me, requires me to grow up and leave, to get a better job elsewhere; cowardice, he says, is to stay put, possumlike, as the world goes on by. But at least my credentials as a San Joaquin Valley loyalist are unimpeachable, and thus my lament over its destruction is genuine."

Hanson lives on the family farm, but no longer actually farms it. "When we all went to the universities, when we abandoned what made us good and embraced what made us comfortable and secure, we lost something essential, knew we lost it and yet chose to lose," he writes. "Material bounty and freedom are so much stronger incentives than sacrifice and character." What was lost by the "we" of this passage, and in Hanson's view by America itself, was the pure hardship of the agrarian life, the yeoman ideal that constituted the country's "last link with the founding fathers of our political and spiritual past," its last line of defense against "market capitalism and entitlement democracy, the final stage of Western culture that is beyond good and evil."

This gets tricky. Notice the way in which the author implicitly frames his indictment of himself and his family for turning away from the pure agrarian life as an indictment of the rest of us, for failing to support that life. Notice, too, that the "destruction" of the San Joaquin Valley, as he sees it, began at the point when the small family farms on the east side of the Valley (the arid west side of the Valley, the part described by William Henry Brewer in the 1860s as a "plain of absolute desolation," belonged to the corporate growers) began giving way first to industrial parks and subdivisions and then to strip malls and meth labs. "Its Golden Age was therefore brief, no more than the beautiful century between 1870 and 1970, when gravity-fed irrigation in hand-dug ditches from the Sierra first turned a weed-infested desert into an oasis of small tree and vine farms and their quiet satellite communities."

This "Golden Age," in other words, began with the arrival of Hanson's own family, and ended with his own adolescence. "Times have changed," as the similarly focused Saxon Brown complained to Billy Roberts in *The Valley of the Moon*. "They've changed even since I was a little girl." There is a further possible mirage here: the San Joaquin Valley's "beautiful century" could have seemed, to those who were actually living it, perhaps not entirely golden: "Here, in this corner of a great nation, here, on the edge of the continent, here, in this valley of the West, far from the great centers, isolated, remote, lost, the great iron hand crushes life from us, crushes liberty and the pursuit of happiness from us. . . . Tell them, five years from now, the story of the fight between the League of the San Joaquin and the railroad and it will not be believed." That was Frank Norris, writing in *The Octopus*, on the slaughter that took place in 1880 at Mussel Slough, now Lucerne, now and then just fifteen miles from Selma, the site of the farmhouse in which six generations of Victor Davis Hanson's family have lived.

"There in my own small town," Hanson tells us in *The Land Was Everything*, "we have torn up vineyards and now have planted the following crops: Wal-Mart, Burger King, Food-4-Less, Baskin-Robbins, Cinema 6, Denny's, Wendy's, Payless, Andersen's Pea Soup, the Holiday Inn, McDonald's, Carl's Jr., Taco Bell, four gas stations, three shopping centers, two videotape stores, and a car wash." In line with the thrust of his argument, Hanson offers this list as evidence of "change," specifically of the moral or spiritual impoverishment to which he believes the loss of the yeoman ethic in the San Joaquin Valley has led. Some readers—those, say, who remain unconvinced that there was ever a yeoman ethic in the San Joaquin Valley to lose—might take from the list evidence of a less elusive impoverishment: the enterprises named are in the main national chains, or franchises, not the kinds of entrepreneurial activity calculated to return either money or opportunity to the community.

According to a study conducted by the Public Policy Institute of California, the poverty rate in the San Joaquin Valley in the year 2000 was in fact twenty-two percent of the population, the highest in the state, which in turn had an overall poverty rate, when adjusted for cost of living, exceeded in the United States only by that of the District of Columbia. This overall California poverty rate began exceeding that of the rest of the nation only in the late 1980s, but being poor in the Central Valley was not a new condition. In 1980, of the ten American metropolitan areas most reliant on public assistance, six were in the Sacramento and San Joaquin Valleys, running south from Redding and Yuba City–Marysville and Stockton straight down through Modesto and Fresno and Visalia. Many assumed California's rising poverty rate to be a function of immigration, and to some degree, in the short term, it was: the foreign-born, particularly those from Southeast Asia and Hispanic America, who did have the highest rate of poverty in the state.

In the Central Valley, however, immigration did not

tell the whole story. In 1998, Tulare County began paying its welfare clients the cost of relocating in other states, providing an average of $2,300 a client to rent a U-Haul van and buy gas and stay in motels en route and pay first-and-last-month rent on a place to live once they get there. This policy, which also includes e-mailing job applications and mining the Internet for apartment rentals, has since been adopted by four other San Joaquin counties, Kings, Madera, Fresno, and Kern. In June 2001 and June 2002, reporters from first *The New York Times* and then *The Washington Post* interviewed samplings of these relocated clients. There were David Langley and his wife and child, who moved from Visalia to Colorado, as did Jackie and Michael Foster, "with their year-old red-haired son." There was Lorrie Gedert, who moved with her two daughters from Ivanhoe, about ten miles outside Visalia, to Little Rock. There were Gloria and Nathan Dickerson, who moved with their two children, Emily and Drake, from Visalia to Ocala, Florida. There were Richard and Zena White, who moved from Fresno to Slidell, Louisiana, where, according to the *Post,* both are now working full-time, "Zena as an assistant manager at a Chevron gas station and Richard as a shift manager at McDonald's." What first strikes the reader of these reports is that the names of the former Californians interviewed do not uniformly suggest recent immigration from Southeast Asia or Hispanic America. What next strikes the reader is that even such marginal jobs as assistant manager at the Chevron station and shift manager at the McDonald's appear to have been unobtainable in the San

Joaquin Valley, here where the vineyards got torn up so the Wal-Marts and the Burger Kings and the Taco Bells could grow, here, as Frank Norris saw it in 1901, *in this corner of a great nation, here, on the edge of the continent, here, in this valley of the West, far from the great centers, isolated, remote, lost.*

3

FOR most of my life California felt rich to me: that was the point of it, that was the promise, the reward for having left the past on the Sweetwater, the very texture of the place. This was by no means to say that I believed all or even most Californians to be rich, only to suggest that the fact of having no money seemed to me to lack, in California, the immutable gravity that characterized the condition elsewhere. It was not designed to be a life sentence. You were meant, if you were a Californian, to know how to lash together a corral with bark, you were meant to know how to tent a raft and live on the river, you were meant to show spirit, kill the rattlesnake, keep moving. There were in California a lot of "dead brokes," Henry George had pointed out in 1868, in a passage from "What the Railroad Will Bring Us" that got read to me (rather selectively, in retrospect) by my grandfather, "but there never was a better country to be 'broken' in, and where almost every man, even the most successful, had been in the same position, it did not involve the humiliation and loss of hope which attaches to utter poverty in older and more settled communities."

That I should have continued, deep into adult life, to think of California as I was told as a child that it had been in 1868 suggests a confusion of some magnitude, but there it was. *It's not a word we use,* my mother had said about class. *It's not the way we think.* Only in the 1980s did certain facts—two of them, not unrelated—manage to penetrate what was clearly a fairly tenacious wish not to examine whatever it was I needed to believe. The first fact, which entered my attention as an almost personal affront, was that California no longer felt rich enough to adequately fund its education system. The second, or corollary, fact was that there seemed to be many towns in California—including towns I knew, towns I thought of as my own interior landscape, towns I had thought I understood, towns in the Sacramento and San Joaquin Valleys—so impoverished in spirit as well as in fact that the only way their citizens could think to reverse their fortunes was by getting themselves a state prison. Since the building and staffing of new prisons were major reasons why California no longer felt rich enough to adequately fund its education system, this second fact initially presented itself as an even deeper affront than the first, evidence that a "new" California had finally and fatally sold out the old.

Then I remembered, then I realized.

We were seeing nothing "new" here.

We were seeing one more version of making our deal with the Southern Pacific.

We were seeing one more version of making our bed with the federal government.

We were seeing one more enthusiastic fall into a familiar California error, that of selling the future of the place we lived to the highest bidder, which was in this instance the California Correctional Peace Officers Association.

The California Correctional Peace Officers Association is the prison guards' union, a 29,000-member force that has maintained for some years now the most effective lobbying operation in Sacramento. In the 1998 election cycle, for example, the union funneled over two million dollars to Grey Davis's gubernatorial campaign and another three million dollars to various other candidates and propositions. "All I've ever asked is that we get to play in the ballpark with all the big guys and gals out there," Don Novey told *The Los Angeles Times* in 2000. Don Novey is the former guard at Folsom State Prison who became in 1980 the president of the California Correctional Peace Officers Association. "They call us the 800-pound gorilla. But we're just taking care of our own like everybody else." Don Novey refers to those who consider the need for new prisons an arguable proposition as "the other element." He gave $75,000 to the opponent of a state senator who had once spoken against a prison bond issue. "If Don Novey ran the contractors' union," a Republican strategist told the *Times,* "there'd be a bridge over every puddle in the state." The prison guards were in California the political muscle behind the victims' rights movement. The prison guards were in California the

political muscle behind the 1994 "three strikes" legislation and initiative, the act that mandated a sentence of
twenty-five years to life for any third felony conviction,
even for crimes as minor as growing a marijuana plant on
a windowsill or shoplifting a bottle of Ripple. The prison
guards were the political muscle that had by the year
2000 made the California corrections system, with thirty-
three penitentiaries and 162,000 inmates, the largest in
the western hemisphere.

Incarceration was not always a growth industry in
California. In 1852 there was only San Quentin, by 1880
there was also Folsom. During the 104 years that followed, a century during which the population of California increased from 865,000 to 25,795,000 people, the
state found need for only ten additional facilities, most of
them low or medium security. It was only in 1984, four
years after Don Novey took over the union, that the new
max and supermax prisons began rolling online, Solano in
1984, "New Folsom" (a quarter mile removed from "Old
Folsom") in 1986, Avenal and Ione and Stockton and
San Diego in 1987, Corcoran and Blythe in 1988, Pelican
Bay in 1989, Chowchilla in 1990, Wasco in 1991, Calipatria in 1992, Lancaster and Imperial and Centinela and
Delano in 1993, Coalinga and a second prison at Blythe in
1994, second prisons at both Susanville and Chowchilla
in 1995, Soledad in 1996, a second prison at Corcoran in
1997.

Delano, the town in the San Joaquin between Tulare
and Bakersfield that became synonymous outside California with Cesar Chavez's farmworkers' union, still

yearns for its own second prison, "New Delano," to be built just across the road from what is already called "Old Delano," the ten-year-old North Kern State Prison. Mendota, west of Fresno and south of Chowchilla, still waits for what was to have been its privately built and operated prison, on which construction was begun and then postponed by the Nashville-based Corrections Corporation of America, which had hit a snag trying to contract with the state for prisoners to fill the $100 million maximum-security prison it had already built in the Mojave desert. "They can build whatever prisons they want," Don Novey had said to this point. "But the hell if they're going to run them."

That these prisons should remain the objects of abject civic desire is curious, since they have not actually enriched the towns that got them. A new prison creates jobs, but few of those jobs go to local hires. The Department of Corrections allows that it imports half the "corrections workers" in any new prison, but "tries" to hire the rest from the community. Opponents to "New Delano" point out that only seven to nine percent of the jobs at these new prisons have typically been local hires, and that the local hires get the low-paid service jobs. Of the 1,600 projected jobs at "New Delano," only 72 would be local hires. There are, moreover, costs, both economic and social: when the families of inmates move into a prison town, they not only strain the limited resources of local schools and social service agencies but bring emotionally stressed children into the community and school system. "The students are all very high risk," a school official in

Lassen County, where Susanville is located, told *The Los Angeles Times*. "They come from single-parent homes. They're latchkey kids, often on AFDC. It's very obvious they're from a whole different area. It creates societal conflicts. The child does not fit in."

It was 1993 when the California Department of Corrections activated its first "death fence," at Calipatria. It was 1994 when the second "death fence" was activated, at Lancaster, carrying a charge of 650 milliamperes, almost ten times the voltage required to cause instant death. "What the fence does is take out the human-error part," the warden at Lancaster was quoted as having said, explaining that the million-dollar fences would save money in the long run because armed officers could be removed from prison gun towers. "The fence never goes to sleep. It doesn't go to the bathroom. It doesn't do any of those things. It's always working." It was also 1994 when standardized testing of reading skills among California fourth-graders placed them last in the nation, below Mississippi, tied only with Louisiana. It was 1995 when, for the first time, California spent more on its prisons than on its two university systems, the ten campuses of the University of California and the twenty-four campuses of California State University.

Through most of my life I would have interpreted the growth of the prison system and the diminution of the commitment to public education as evidence of how California had "changed." Only recently did I come to see them as the opposite, evidence of how California had "not changed," and to understand "change" itself as one of the culture's most enduring misunderstandings about itself.

4

"The American community in early California fairly represented, as we shall see, the average national culture and character. But no other part of our land was ever so rapidly peopled as was California in the first golden days. Nowhere else were we Americans more affected than here, in our lives and conduct, by the feeling that we stood in the position of conquerors in a new land. Nowhere else, again, were we ever before so long forced by circumstance to live at the mercy of a very wayward chance, and to give to even our most legitimate business a dangerously speculative character. Nowhere else were we driven so hastily to improvise a government for a large body of strangers; and nowhere else did fortune so nearly deprive us for a little time of our natural devotion to the duties of citizenship. We Americans therefore showed, in early California, new failings and new strength. We exhibited a novel degree of carelessness and overhastiness, an extravagant trust in luck, a previously unknown blindness to our social duties, and an indifference to the rights of foreigners, whereof we cannot be proud. But we also showed our best national traits—traits that went far to atone for our faults. As a body, our pioneer community in California was persistently cheerful, energetic, courageous, and teachable. In a few years it had repented of its graver faults, it had endured with charming good humor their severest penalties, and it was ready to begin with fresh devotion the work whose true importance it had now at length learned—the work of building a well-organized, permanent, and progressive State on the Pacific Coast. In this work it has been engaged ever since."

—Josiah Royce,
California: A Study of American Character, 1886

JUST east of Sacramento, off Kilgore Road in what is now Rancho Cordova, a town with a population of almost fifty thousand that exists only because Aerojet General began manufacturing rockets there after World War Two, there is a three-acre family graveyard, the Matthew Kilgore Cemetery, its gates long gone, its two-hundred-some graves overgrown and many of its stone markers, a few of which are dated as recently as the 1970s, overturned. Two of my great-great-great-grandparents, Matthew Kilgore and his wife Massa McGuire Kilgore, were buried there, Massa Kilgore in 1876, Matthew Kilgore in 1882. When I was in high school and college and later I would sometimes drive out there, park the car and sit on the fender and read, but after the day I noticed, as I was turning off the ignition, a rattlesnake slide from a broken stone into the dry grass, I never again got out of the car.

In the 1980s, when the condition of the Kilgore Cemetery had become a matter of local concern (vandals had dug up a body and stolen its head), the president of the Rancho Cordova Chamber of Commerce appealed to "Cordovans" (residents of Rancho Cordova, in other words "new people") to join a volunteer effort to clean up the beer bottles and debris left by trespassers. "There are a lot of residents who would like to see this historic site preserved as it deserves to be," he was quoted as having said in the newspaper story my mother clipped and sent to me in Los Angeles.

I asked, when my mother and I next spoke, if the family—the seventy-some of my father's cousins who annually attended the Kilgore Family Reunion in McKinley Park in East Sacramento, say—was joining the effort to clean up the Kilgore Cemetery.

The family, my mother said, did not own the Kilgore Cemetery.

It occurred to me that neither did the president of the Rancho Cordova Chamber of Commerce own the Kilgore Cemetery, but I opted to go in a different direction. I asked how exactly it had come to pass that the family did not own the Kilgore Cemetery.

"I presume somebody sold it," my mother said.

I thought about this.

I also thought about having seen the rattlesnake slide from the broken stone into the grass.

I had seen the rattlesnake but I had failed to get out of

the car and kill it, thereby violating, in full awareness that
I was so doing, what my grandfather had told me was "the
code of the West."

If "not killing the rattlesnake" violated "the code of
the West," how about "selling the cemetery"? Would that
qualify? Not surprisingly, the Kilgore Cemetery makes an
appearance of a kind in *Run River.* Lily's father, Walter
Knight, after he misses a curve on the river road and
drowns trapped in his car, is buried in what is described as
a small family cemetery where the last previous burial had
taken place in 1892. The burial is described from Lily's
point of view: "There was a certain comfort in the
unkempt graveyard. Dried grass obscured the markers,
and the wings had been broken years before from the stone
angels guarding the rusted wire gate; there was about the
place none of the respect for death implicit in a well-
tended plot."

Could this have been what I thought letting the Kilgore Cemetery go to ruin demonstrated? Some admirable
wagons-west refusal to grant death its dominion? The
idealization of the small family cemetery in *Run River*
continues: "Once, a long time before, Walter Knight had
brought Lily to see this graveyard. He had made her trace
out with her finger the letters on the stones, the names
and their dates, until she found the small, rough stone
which marked the oldest grave." This "oldest grave" was
that of a child not yet two, the first family member to die
in California. "I think nobody owns land until their dead
are in it," Walter Knight had said to Lily on this occasion.
"Sometimes I think this whole valley belongs to me," Lily

had said, and her father had responded sharply: "It does, you hear me? We made it."

Had I known when I was writing *Run River* that the Kilgore Cemetery had been or would be sold, was this the rationalization I would have worked out? Our dead were in it, so we owned it? Our deal, so we could sell it? Or would I have somehow managed to incorporate "selling the cemetery" into my bill of particulars against the "new people," against the "changes"? At what point exactly might I have asked: was it new people who sold the cemetery? Was it new people who ploughed under and grazed out the grass that could be tied over the saddle? How would Josiah Royce have construed "selling the cemetery"? "Novel degree of carelessness"? "Previously unknown blindness to social duties"? Or "building a well-organized, permanent, and progressive State on the Pacific Coast"? Or was that the same thing?

From the 1870s to the 1920s, according to Richard W. Fox's 1978 study *So Far Disordered in Mind: Insanity in California 1870–1930,* California had a higher rate of commitment for insanity than any other state in the nation, a disproportion most reasonably explained, Fox suggests, "by the zeal with which California state officials sought to locate, detain, and treat not only those considered 'mentally ill,' but also a wide variety of other deviants—including, as state hospital physicians put it, 'imbeciles, dotards, idiots, drunkards, simpletons, fools,' and 'the aged, the vagabond, the helpless.'" Not only did

California have this notably higher rate of commitment but the institutions to which it committed its citizens differed fundamentally from those in the East, where the idea of how to deal with insanity had been from the beginning medicalized, based on regimes—however more honored in the breach—of treatment and therapy. The idea of how to deal with insanity in California began and ended with detention.

So broad were the standards for committal, and so general was the inclination to let the state take care of what might in another culture have been construed as a family burden, that even many of the doctors who ran the system were uneasy. As early as 1862, according to *So Far Disordered in Mind,* the resident physician at the Stockton State Asylum for the Insane complained of receiving patients "who, if affected in their minds at all, it is the weakness of old age, or intemperance, or perhaps most commonly both together." In 1870, the federal census classified one in every 489 Californians as insane. By 1880, the rate had risen to one in 345. After 1903, when the rate had reached one in 260 and the asylums had passed capacity, the notion of sterilizing inmates gained currency, the idea being that a certain number could then be released without danger of reproducing. Sterilization, or "asexualization," of inmates, which was legalized in some other states as early as 1907, was made legal in California in 1909. By 1917, the right of the state to sterilize had been extended twice, first to cases in which the patient did not agree to the procedure, then to cases in which the patient had not even been necessarily diagnosed with a hereditary or incurable disorder, but only with "perversion or marked departures from normal mentality." By the end of 1920, of the 3,233 sterilizations for insanity or feeblemindedness performed to that date throughout the United States, 2,558, or seventy-nine percent, had taken place in California.

What was arresting in this pattern of commitment was the extent to which it diverged from the California sense of itself as loose, less socially rigid than the rest of the country, more adaptable, more tolerant of difference. When Fox analyzed the San Francisco commitment records for the years 1906 to 1929, he found that the majority of those hospitalized, fifty-nine percent, had been committed not because they were violent, not because they presented a threat to others or to themselves, but simply because they had been reported, sometimes by a police officer but often by a neighbor or relative, to exhibit "odd or peculiar behavior." In 1914, for example, San Francisco medical examiners granted the wish of a woman to commit her thirty-seven-year-old unmarried sister, on the grounds that the sister, despite her "quiet and friendly" appearance during detention, had begun "to act silly, lost interest in all things which interest women, could no longer crochet correctly as formerly, takes no interest in anything at present." In 1915, a forty-year-old clerk was committed because "for three weeks he has been annoying the City Registrar, calling every day and insisting that he is a Deputy." In 1922, a twenty-three-year-old divorcée was committed after a neighbor reported that she was "lazy, slovenly, careless of personal appearance, stays away from home for days, neglecting self and consorting with men." The same year, a forty-eight-year-old pianist was committed on the grounds that "she has been irresponsible for years; has been a source of great annoyance to many institutions such as Y.W.C.A. Association, churches, etc."

The apparently pressing need to commit so many and in many cases such marginally troubled Californians to indefinite custodial detention seems not at the time to have struck their fellow citizens as an excessive lust for social control. Nor did these fellow citizens appear to see their readiness to slough off bothersome relatives and neighbors as a possible defect in their own socialization. Madness, it became convenient to believe quite early on, came with the territory, on the order of earthquakes. The first State Lunatic Asylum in California, that at Stockton, was established in 1853 specifically to treat those believed to have been driven mad by the goldfields. According to an 1873 State Board of Health report, this endemic madness had to do with "the speculative and gambling spirit" of the California settlement. It had to do with "heterogeneous elements," it had to do with "change of climate, habits, and modes of life," it had to do with being "isolated, without sympathy, and deprived of all home influences." California itself, then, according to its own Board of Health, was "well-calculated to break some link in reason's chain, and throw into confusion even the best balanced properties of mind."

I have on my desk a copy of the 1895 *California Blue Book, or State Roster,* family detritus, salvaged from a Good

Will box during a move of my mother's. I assumed at the time I retrieved it that the roster had been my grand-father's but I see now that the bookplate reads "Property of Chas. F. Johnson, Bakersfield, Calif., No. 230," in other words the detritus of someone else's family. The book is illustrated with etchings and photographs, a startling number of which feature what were in 1895 the state's five asylums for the insane, huge Victorian structures that appear to have risen from the deserts and fields of California's rural counties in a solitude more punitive than therapeutic. Among the illustrations are the facts, in neat columns: there were at the Napa State Asylum for the Insane thirty-five "Attendants," each of whom received an annual salary of $540. All were identified by name. There were, listed under the "Attendants" and also identified by name, sixty "Assistant Attendants," thirteen of whom received $480 a year and the rest $420. There were on the staff at the State Insane Asylum at Agnews, in Santa Clara County, more "Cooks" and "Assistant Cooks" and "Bakers" and "Assistant Bakers" than there appear to have been doctors (the only doctors listed are the "Medical Director," at $3,500, and two "Assistant Physicians," at $2,500 and $2,100 respectively), but the staff roster also includes—a note that chills by the dolorous entertainments it suggests—one "Musician, and Assistant Attendant," budgeted at $60 a year more than the other, presumably unmusical, Assistant Attendants.

These places survived through my childhood and adolescence into my adult life, sources of a fear more potent even than that of drowning in the rivers (drowning meant you had misread the river, drowning made sense, drowning you could negotiate), the fear of being sent away—no, worse—"put away." There was near Sacramento an asylum where I was periodically taken with my Girl Scout troop to exhibit for the inmates our determined cheerfulness while singing rounds, nine-year-olds with merit badges on our sleeves pressed into service as Musicians and Assistant Attendants. *White coral bells upon a slender stalk,* we sang in the sunroom, trying not to make eye contact, *lilies of the valley line your garden walk.* I could not have known at nine that my grandmother's sister, who arrived lost in melancholia to live with us after her husband died, would herself die in the asylum at Napa, but the possibility that such a fate could strike at random was the air we breathed.

Oh don't you wish that you could hear them ring, we sang, one by one faltering, only the strongest or most oblivious among us able to keep the round going in the presence of the put away, the now intractably lost, the abandoned, *that will happen only when the angels sing.* If it was going to be us or them, which of us in that sunroom would not have regressed in Royce's view to that "novel degree of carelessness," that "previously unknown blindness to social duties"? Which of us in that sunroom could not have abandoned the orphaned Miss Gilmore and her brother on the Little Sandy? Which of us in that sunroom did not at some level share in the shameful but entrenched conviction that to be weak or bothersome was to warrant abandonment? Which of us in that sunroom would not see the rattlesnake and fail to kill it? Which of us in that sunroom would not sell the cemetery? Were not such abandonments the very heart and soul of the crossing story? Jettison weight? Keep moving? Bury the dead in the trail and run the wagons over it? Never dwell on what got left behind, never look back at all? *Remember,* Virginia Reed had warned attentive California children, we who had been trained since virtual infancy in the horrors she had survived, *never take no cutoffs and hurry along as fast as you can.* Once on a drive to Lake Tahoe I found myself impelled to instruct my brother's small children in the dread lesson of the Donner Party, just in case he had thought to spare them. "Don't worry about it," another attentive California child, Patricia Hearst, recalled having told herself during the time she was locked in a closet by her kidnappers. "Don't examine your feelings. Never examine your feelings—they're no help at all."

Part Four

I

To me as a child, the State was the world as I knew it, and I pictured other States and countries as pretty much "like this." I never felt the warm, colorful force of the beauty of California until I had gone away and come back over my father's route: dull plains; hot, dry desert; the night of icy mountains; the dawning foothills breaking into the full day of sunshine in the valley; and last, the sunset through the Golden Gate. And I came to it by railroad, comfortably, swiftly. My father, who plodded and fought or worried the whole long hard way at oxen pace, always paused when he recalled how they turned over the summit and waded down, joyously, into the amazing golden sea of sunshine—he would pause, see it again as he saw it then, and say, "I saw that this was the place to live."

—Lincoln Steffens,
The Autobiography of Lincoln Steffens

MY MOTHER died on May 15, 2001, in Monterey, two weeks short of her ninety-first birthday. The preceding afternoon I had talked to her on the telephone from New York and she had hung up midsentence, a way of saying goodbye so characteristic of her—especially by way of allowing her callers to economize on what she still called "long distance"—that it did not occur to me until morning, when my brother called, that in this one last instance she had been just too frail to keep the connection.

Maybe not just too frail.

Maybe too aware of what could be the import of this particular goodbye.

Flying to Monterey I had a sharp apprehension of the many times before when I had, like Lincoln Steffens, "come back," flown west, followed the sun, each time experiencing a lightening of spirit as the land below opened up, the checkerboards of the midwestern plains giving way to the vast empty reach between the Rockies and the Sierra Nevada; then *home, there, where I was from, me,* California. It would be a while before I realized that "me" is what we think when our parents die, even at my age, *who will look out for me now, who will remember me as I was, who will know what happens to me now, where will I be from.*

I n the aftermath of my mother's death I found myself thinking a good deal about the confusions and contradictions in California life, many of which she had herself embodied. She despised, for example, the federal government and its "giveaways," but saw no contradiction between this view and her reliance on my father's military reserve status to make free use of Air Force doctors and pharmacies, or to shop at the commissaries and exchanges of whatever military installation she happened to be near. She thought of the true California spirit as one of unfettered individualism, but carried the idea of individual rights to dizzying and often punitive lengths. She definitely aimed for an appearance of being "stern," a word she seemed to think synonymous with what was not then called "parenting." As a child herself in the upper Sacramento Valley she had watched men hung in front of the courthouse. When John Kennedy was assassinated she insisted that Lee Harvey Oswald had "every right" to assassinate him, that Jack Ruby in turn had "every right" to kill Lee Harvey Oswald, and that any breakdown of natural order in the event had been on the part of the Dallas police, who had failed to exercise their own right, which was "to shoot Ruby on the spot." When I introduced her to my future husband, she advised him immediately that he would find her political beliefs so far to the right that he would think her "the original little old lady in tennis shoes." At Christmas that year he gave her the entire John Birch library, dozens of call-to-action pamphlets, boxed. She was delighted, amused, displaying the pamphlets to everyone who came by the house that season, but to the best of my knowledge she never opened one.

She was passionately opinionated on a number of points that reflected, on examination, no belief she actually held. She thought of herself as an Episcopalian, as her mother had been. She was married at Trinity Episcopal Pro-Cathedral in Sacramento. She had me christened there. She buried her mother there. My brother and I had her own funeral service at Saint John's Episcopal Chapel in Monterey, a church she had actually attended only two or three times but favored as an idea not only because it was a "California" church (it was built in the 1880s by Charles Crocker and C. P. Huntington on the grounds of the Southern Pacific's Del Monte Hotel) but also because the litany used was that from the 1928, as opposed to the revised, *Book of Common Prayer.* Yet she had herself at age twelve refused outright to be confirmed an Episcopalian: she had gone through the instruction and been presented to the bishop, but, when asked for the usual rote affirmation of a fairly key doctrinal point, had declared resoundingly, as if it were a debate, that she found herself "incapable of believing" that Christ was the son of God. By the time of my own confirmation, she had further hardened this position. "The only church I could possibly go to would be Unitarian," she announced when my grandmother asked why she never went to church with us.

"Eduene," my grandmother said, a soft keening. "How can you say that."

"I *have* to say it, if I want to be honest," my mother said, the voice of sweet reason. "Since I don't believe that Christ is the son of God."

My grandmother brightened, seeing space for resolution. "Then it's fine," she said. "Because nobody has to believe all *that.*"

Only in recent years did I come to realize that many of these dramatically pronounced opinions of my mother's were defensive, her own version of her great-grandmother's "fixed and settled principles, aims and motives in life," a barricade against some deep apprehension of meaninglessness. There had been glimpses of this apprehension all along, overlooked by me, my own barricade. She did not see a point in making beds, for example, since "they just get slept in again." Nor did she see a point in dusting, since dust just returned. "What difference does it make," she would often say, by way of ending a discussion of whether an acquaintance should leave her husband, say, or whether a cousin should drop out of school and become a manicurist. "What difference does it make," five words that had come to chill me at the bone, was what she said when I pressed her on the point about selling the cemetery. On the Good Friday after her own mother died she happened to be driving across the country with a friend from Sacramento. At the place where they stopped for dinner there had been no fish on the menu, only meat. "I took one bite and I thought of Mother and I wanted to throw up," my mother said when she arrived at my apartment in New York a few days later. Her mother, she said, would never eat meat on Good Friday. Her mother did not like to cook fish, but she would get a crab and crack it. I was about to suggest that cracked Dungeness crab was hard to come by on the average midwestern road trip, but before I could speak I noticed that she was crying. "What difference does it make," she said finally.

I had seen my mother cry only once before. The first time had been during World War Two, on a downtown street in some town where my father was stationed, Tacoma or Durham or Colorado Springs. My brother and I had been left in the car while our mother went into the military housing office that dealt with dependents. The office was crowded, women and children leaning against the plate glass windows and spilling outside. When our mother came back out onto the sidewalk she was crying: it seemed to be the end of some rope, one day too many on which there would be no place for us to stay.

The blank dreariness, Sarah Royce wrote.

Without house or home.

When she got into the car her eyes were dry and her expression was determinedly cheerful. "It's an adventure," she said. "It's wartime, it's history, you children will be thankful you got to see all this." In one of those towns we finally got a room in a hotel, with a shared bathtub, into which she poured a bottle of pine disinfectant every day before bathing us. In Durham we had one room, with kitchen privileges, in the house of a fundamentalist preacher and his family who sat on the porch after dinner and ate peach ice cream, each from his or her own quart carton. The preacher's daughter had a full set of *Gone With the Wind* paper dolls, off limits to me. It was in Durham where the neighborhood children crawled beneath the back stoop and ate the dirt, scooping it up with a cut raw potato and licking it off, craving some element their diet lacked.

Pica.

I knew the word even then, because my mother told me. "Poor children do it," she said, with the same determinedly cheerful expression. "In the South. You never would have learned that in Sacramento."

It was in Durham where my mother noticed my brother reaching for something through the bars of his playpen and froze, unable to move, because what he was reaching for was a copperhead. The copperhead moved on, possibly another instance of the "providential interposition" that had spared my mother's great-great-grandfather from the mad dog in Georgia.

Something occurs to me as I write this: my mother did not kill the copperhead.

Only once, in Colorado Springs, did we actually end up living in a house of our own—not much of a house, a four-room stucco bungalow, rented furnished, but a house. I had skipped part of first grade because we were moving around and I had skipped second grade because we were moving around but in Colorado Springs we had a house, in Colorado Springs I could go to school. I did. They were already doing multiplication and I had skipped learning how to subtract. Out at the base where my father was stationed pilots kept spiraling down through the high thin Colorado air. The way you knew was that you heard the crash wagons. A classmate told me that her mother did not allow her to play with military trash. My grandmother came by train to visit, bringing as usual material solace, thick blue towels and Helena Rubinstein soap in the shape of apple blossoms. I have snapshots of the two of us in front of the Broadmoor Hotel, my grandmother in a John Fredericks hat, me in a Brownie uniform. "You are just out of luck to be home because it's so nice and warm here," I wrote to her when she was gone. The letter, which I found with my mother's snapshots of the period, is decorated with gold and silver stars and cutout Christmas trees, suggesting that I had been trying hard for the upbeat. "But Mommy heard a girl say on the base that 'Remember last New Year's? It was eighteen below, and we had just this kind of weather.' We have a blue spruce Christmas tree. Jimmy and me are going to a party the 23rd at the base. They have a new name for the base. It's Peterson field."

I remember that my mother made me give the apple-blossom soap to the wife of a departing colonel, a goodbye present. I remember that she encouraged me to build many of those corrals that Californians were meant to know how to build, branches lashed together with their own stripped bark, ready for any loose livestock that might come our way, one of many frontier survival techniques I have never had actual occasion to use. I remember that once when we were snowbound she taught me how to accept and decline formal invitations, a survival technique from a different daydream: *Miss Joan Didion accepts with pleasure the kind invitation of, Miss Joan Didion regrets that she is unable to accept the kind invitation of.* Another time when we were snowbound she gave me several old copies of *Vogue,* and pointed out in one of them an announcement of the competition *Vogue* then had for college seniors, the Prix de Paris, first prize a job in *Vogue*'s Paris or New York office.

You could win that, she said. When the time comes. You could win that and live in Paris. Or New York. Wherever you wanted. But *definitely* you could win it.

A dozen-plus years later, my senior year at Berkeley, I did win it, and drove to Sacramento with the telegram from *Vogue* in my bag. I had found the yellow envelope with the glassine window slipped under my apartment door when I got back from a class that afternoon. *We are delighted to inform you,* the little strips of yellow tape read. *Miss Jessica Daves, Editor-in-Chief, Vogue.* When I showed the telegram to my mother I reminded her that it had been her idea in the first place.

"Really?" she said, doubtful.

This calls for a drink, my father said, his solution, as hanging up was my mother's solution, to any moment when emotion seemed likely to surface.

Colorado Springs, I said, prompting her. When we were snowbound.

"Imagine your remembering," she said.

I see now that World War Two was our own Big Sandy, Little Sandy, Humboldt Sink.

I magine your remembering.
    Something else I remembered: I remembered her telling me that when the war was over we would *all* go to live in Paris. *Toute la famille.* Paris had not yet been liberated but she already had a plan: my father was to reinvent himself as an architect, study architecture at the Sorbonne on the G.I. Bill. To this end she tried to teach me the French she had learned at Lowell High School in San Francisco.

Pourquoi did we never go to live in Paris?

Je ne sais pas.

A few years after the war ended, when we were again living in Sacramento, I asked this question. My mother said that we had never gone to live in Paris because my father felt an obligation to his family to remain in Sacramento. I recall wondering how much of the plan she had actually discussed with him, since I had never been able to quite bring the picture of my father dropping everything and starting over in Paris into clear focus. The problem in the picture was not that he was risk-averse. Risk was in fact our bread and butter, risk was what put the lamb chops on the table. He had supported my mother and me during the Depression by playing poker with older and more settled acquaintances at the Sutter Club, a men's club in Sacramento to which he did not belong. Right now, after the war, he was supporting my mother and brother and me by buying houses and pieces of property with no money to speak of, then leveraging them, and buying some more. His idea of a relaxing way to make a payment was to drive to Nevada and shoot craps all night.

No.

"Risk" he definitely would have gone for.

The problem in the picture was "Paris."

One of the few perfectly clear points in his belief system (there was much that remained opaque) was the conviction that France, where he had never been, was a worthless country peopled exclusively by the devious, the corrupt, the frivolous, and the collaborating. The name "Didion," he insisted, was not French but German, the name of an ancestor who, although German, "happened to live in Alsace after the French took it over." The first time I went to Paris I sent him a page from a telephone book on which many apparently French Parisians named "Didion" were listed, but he never mentioned it.

One element in my mother's version of the chimerical Paris adventure did hold up: it was true that my father felt an obligation to his family to remain in Sacramento. The reason he felt this obligation had been distilled, within the family and over the years, into a plausible sequence of events, a story so reasonable that it seemed unconvincing, a kind of cartoon. Here was the story: when his mother was dying of influenza in 1918 she had told him to take care of his younger brother, and when his brother lost an eye in a fireworks accident my father thought he had failed. In fact whatever unfulfilled and unfulfillable obligation he felt was less identifiable than that. There was about him a sadness so pervasive that it colored even those many moments when he seemed to be having a good time. He had many friends. He played golf, he played tennis, he played poker, he seemed to enjoy parties. Yet he could be in the middle of a party at our own house, sitting at the piano—playing "Darktown Strutter's Ball," say, or "Alexander's Ragtime Band," a bourbon highball always within reach—and the tension he transmitted would seem so great that I would have to leave, run to my room and close the door.

It was during my first year at Berkeley when the physical manifestations of this tension became sufficiently troubling that he was referred to Letterman Hospital, at the Presidio in San Francisco, to undergo a series of tests. I am unsure how long he spent at Letterman, but it was a period covering some weeks or months. My mother would drive down from Sacramento on the weekends, either Saturday or Sunday, and pick me up at the Tri Delt house in Berkeley. We would cross the Bay Bridge and go out to the Presidio and pick up my father for lunch. I remember that all he would eat that year were oysters, raw. I remember that after the oysters we would spend the rest of the afternoon driving—not back into the city, because he did not like San Francisco, but through Golden Gate Park, down the beach, over into Marin County, anywhere he was likely to see a pickup baseball game he could stop and watch. I remember that at the end of the afternoon he would instruct my mother to drop him not at the Presidio but at the southwesternmost end of Golden Gate Park, so that he could walk back to the hospital along the beach. Sometimes during the week he would walk across the Golden Gate Bridge, visit a cousin at his Sausalito office, and walk back. Once I walked across the bridge with him. I remember that it swayed. In his letters to my mother he dismissed the Letterman psychiatrists as "the mind guys," or sometimes "the mind-over-matter guys," but a year or so before he died, in his eighties, he told me that there had been "this woman doctor" at Letterman who had been "actually very helpful" to him. "We talked about my mother," he said. It was several years after he died before I was able to fully articulate what could not have escaped either my or my mother's fixedly narrowed attention on those weekend afternoons in 1953: those were bad walks for someone under observation for depression.

I t occurs to me how brave he must have been, to make those walks and come back.

It also occurs to me how brave my mother must have been, to drive back alone to Sacramento while he made those walks.

M y father died in December of 1992. A few months later, in March, I happened to drive my mother from Monterey to Berkeley, where we were to spend a few nights at the Claremont Hotel and I was to speak at a University of California Charter Day ceremony.

"Are we on the right road," my mother had asked again and again as we drove up 101.

I had repeatedly assured her that we were, at last pointing out an overhead sign: *101 North.*

"Then where did it all go," she had asked.

She meant where did Gilroy go, where was the Milias Hotel, where could my father eat short ribs now. She meant where did San Juan Bautista go, why was it no longer so sweetly remote as it had been on the day of my wedding there in 1964. She meant where had San Benito and Santa Clara Counties gone as she remembered them, the coastal hills north of Salinas, the cattle grazing, the familiar open vista that had been relentlessly replaced (during the year, two years, three, the blink of the eye during which she had been caring for my father) by mile after mile of pastel subdivisions and labyrinthine exits and entrances to freeways that had not previously existed.

For some miles she was silent.

California had become, she said then, "all San Jose."

In the bar at the Claremont that evening someone was playing, as if to reinforce what had become a certain time-travel aspect in our excursion, "Only Make Believe," and "Where or When."

The smile you are smiling you were smiling then—
But I can't remember where or when—

I had last been in the bar at the Claremont in 1955, with the son of a rancher from Mendocino County. I recall that I had my roommate's driver's license and a crème de menthe frappé. Thirty-eight years later, from the platform at the Charter Day ceremony, I glanced at the row where my mother was seated and found her chair empty. When I located her outside she told me that it had been essential to leave. She said that "something terrible" had happened during the academic procession, something that had made her fear that she would "cry in front of everybody." It seemed that she had seen a banner reading "Class of 1931," and had realized that the handful of men strag-gling along behind it (if there were any women she did not mention them) were having trouble walking.

The Class of 1931 had been my father's class at Berke-ley. "They were all old men," my mother said about those few of his former classmates who had made the procession. "They were just like your father." *Frank Reese "Jim" Didion,* the memorial note for my father had read in the alumni magazine. *December 19, in Carmel. A native of Sacramento, where he was active as a real estate investor, he majored in business at Cal and was a member of Chi Phi. He is survived by his wife, Eduene, two children, Joan Didion Dunne '56 and James '62, and four grandchildren, including Steven '88 and Lori '93.* There was no believable comfort I could offer my mother: she was right. They were all old men and it was all San Jose. Child of the crossing story that I was, I left my mother with Lori '93 and took the United redeye from San Francisco to Kennedy, the last plane to land before a storm CNN was calling "The Nor'easter of the Century" closed every airport and highway north of Atlanta. I remembered this abandonment the day she died.

2

I also remembered this one.

Sacramento, July or August, 1971 or 1972.

I had brought Quintana—my daughter, then five or six—to spend a few days with my mother and father. Because it would be 105 at two and 110 before the sun went down, my mother and I decided to take Quintana out to lunch, somewhere with air conditioning.

My father did not believe in air conditioning.

My father in fact believed that Sacramento summers had been too cold since the dams.

We would go downtown, my mother said. We would have lunch in the Redevelopment. Old Sacramento. You haven't even *seen* Old Sacramento, she said.

I asked if she had seen Old Sacramento.

Not exactly, she said. But she definitely wanted to. We would see it together, it would be an adventure.

Quintana was wearing a pinafore, pale green, Liberty lawn.

My mother gave her a big straw hat to wear against the sun.

We drove downtown, we parked, we started walking on what had been Front Street, its view of the

Tower Bridge pretty much constituting the "adventure" part.

The sidewalks in the Redevelopment were wooden, to give the effect of 1850.

Quintana was walking ahead of us.

The lawn pinafore, the big hat, the wooden sidewalk, the shimmer of the heat.

My father's great-grandfather had owned a saloon on Front Street.

I was about to explain this to Quintana—the saloon, the wooden sidewalk, the generations of cousins who had walked just as she was walking down just this street on days just this hot—when I stopped. Quintana was adopted. Any ghosts on this wooden sidewalk were not in fact Quintana's responsibility. This wooden sidewalk did not in fact represent anywhere Quintana was from. Quintana's only attachments on this wooden sidewalk were right now, here, me and my mother.

In fact I had no more attachment to this wooden sidewalk than Quintana did: it was no more than a theme, a decorative effect.

It was only Quintana who was real.

Later it seemed to me that this had been the moment when all of it—the crossing, the redemption, the abandoned rosewood chests, the lost flatware, the rivers I had written to replace the rivers I had left, the twelve generations of circuit riders and county sheriffs and Indian fighters and country lawyers and Bible readers, the two

hundred years of clearings in Virginia and Kentucky and
Tennessee and then the break, the dream of America, the
entire enchantment under which I had lived my life—
began to seem remote.

3

O N the afternoon after our mother's funeral my brother and I divided what few pieces of furniture she still had among her grandchildren, my brother's three children and Quintana. There was not much left; during the previous few years she had been systematically giving away what she had, giving back Christmas presents, jettisoning belongings. I do not remember what Quintana's cousins Kelley and Steven and Lori took. I do remember what Quintana took, because I have seen the pieces since in her apartment in New York. There was an oval Victorian table with a marble top that had come to my mother from some part of the family, I no longer remember which. There was a carved teak chest that had been in my mother and father's bedroom when I was a child. There was a small piecrust table that had been my grandmother's. There was, from among my mother's clothes, an Italian angora cape that she had been wearing ever since my father gave it to her, one Christmas in the late 1940s.

Actually I took the angora cape.

I remembered her wearing it the spring before, at the wedding in Pebble Beach, of my brother's youngest child.

I remembered her wearing it in 1964 at my own wedding, wrapping herself in it for the drive from San Juan Bautista to the reception in Pebble Beach.

A representative from Allied came.

The pieces got tagged for shipment.

I put what I did not want to be thrown away—letters, photographs, clippings, folders and envelopes I could not that day summon up the time or the heart to open—in a large box.

Some weeks later the box arrived at my apartment in New York, where it sat in the dining room for perhaps a month, unopened. Finally I opened it. There were pictures of me on the beach at Carmel in 1936, pictures of me and my brother on the beach at Stinson Beach in 1946, pictures of me and my brother and my rabbit in the snow in Colorado Springs. There were pictures of great-aunts and cousins and great-great-grandparents who could be identified only because our mother, on the evening before she died, had thought to tell the names to my brother, who wrote them on the backing of the frames. There were pictures of my mother as a two-year-old visiting her grandmother in Oregon in 1912, there were pictures of my mother at a Peterson Field barbecue in 1943, a young woman in her early thirties wearing flowers in her hair as she makes hamburgers. There was an unframed watercolor of my grandmother's. There were letters my grandmother's brother Jim, like her father a merchant sea captain, had sent her in 1918 from England, where his ship, the S.S. *Armenia,* was in drydock at Southampton after having been torpedoed. There were letters my father had written to his own father in 1928, from a summer job on a construction crew outside Crescent City—my father asking, in letter after letter, if his father could please put in a word for him with an acquaintance who did the hiring for the State Fair jobs, a plea I happen to know was in vain.

I know this because I once wanted my father to make the same call for me.

My mother had told me to forget asking him, because *he's just like his own father, everybody in Sacramento picks up the phone to get their children jobs at the Fair but your father and his father never will, they won't ask for favors.*

There were also letters from me, letters I had written my mother from Berkeley, from the time I went down for summer school in 1952, making up credits between high school and college, until the time I graduated in 1956. These letters were in many ways unsettling, even dispiriting, in that I both recognized myself and did not. *Have never been so depressed as when I got back here Sunday night,* one of the first letters reads, from the summer of 1952. *I keep thinking about Sacramento and what people are doing. I got a letter from Nancy—she misses Sacramento too. They saw "The King and I," "Where's Charley," "Guys and Dolls," and "Pal Joey." A woman committed suicide by jumping out a window across from the Waldorf while they were there. Nancy said it was terrible, they had to clean up the street with fire hoses.*

Nancy was my best friend from Sacramento, traveling with her parents (this is only a guess, but an informed one, since another letter to my mother that summer mentions having "heard from Nancy who is at the Greenbrier and so bored") before beginning Stanford.

Nancy and I had known each other since we were five, when we had been in the same ballet class at Miss Marion Hall's dancing school in Sacramento.

In fact there was also, in the box that came from my mother's house, a program for a recital of that very ballet class: *Joan Didion and Nancy Kennedy,* the program read. *"Les Petites."* There were also in the box many photographs of Nancy and me: modeling children's clothes in a charity fashion show, wearing matching corsages around our wrists at a high-school dance, standing on the lawn outside Nancy's house on the day of her wedding, Nancy in bouffant white, the bridesmaids in pale green organza, all of us smiling.

The last time I saw Nancy was at the Outrigger Canoe Club in Honolulu, during the Christmas season of the Iran hostage crisis. She was at the next table, having dinner with her husband and children. They were laughing and arguing and interrupting just as she and her brothers and her mother and father had laughed and argued and interrupted in the late 1940s and early 1950s, when I would have dinner at their house two or three times a week.

We kissed, we had a drink together, we promised to keep in touch.

A few months later Nancy was dead, of cancer, at Lenox Hill Hospital in New York.

I sent the recital program to Nancy's brother, to send on to her daughter.

I had my grandmother's watercolor framed and sent it to the next oldest of her three granddaughters, my cousin Brenda, in Sacramento.

I closed the box and put it in a closet.

There is no real way to deal with everything we lose.

When my father died I kept moving. When my mother died I could not. The last time I saw her was eight weeks before she died. She had been in the hospital, my brother and I had gotten her home, we had arranged for oxygen and shifts of nurses, we had filled the prescriptions for morphine and Ativan. On the morning Quintana and I were to leave for New York, my mother insisted that we bring her a painted metal box that sat on a small table in her bedroom, a box in which she kept papers she thought might have importance, for example a copy of the deed to a gold mine in El Dorado County that she and her sister had inherited from their father and no longer owned. My brother said that she did not need the box, that he had already extracted any still operable papers and put them in safekeeping. She was insistent. She wanted the metal box. Quintana brought the box and set it on the bed. From it my mother took two pieces of silver flatware, a small ladle and a small serving spoon, each wrapped in smoothed scraps of used tissue paper. She gave the serving spoon to Quintana and the ladle to me. I protested: she had already given me all her silver, I had ladles, she had given me ladles. "Not this one," she said. She pointed out the curve of the handle. It seemed that she had what she called "a special feeling" for the way the handle curved on this particular ladle. It seemed that she found this ladle so satisfying to touch that she had set it aside, kept it. I said that since it gave her pleasure she should continue to keep it. "*Take* it," she said, her voice urgent. "I don't want it lost." I was still pretending that she would get through the Sierra before the snows fell. She was not.

A NOTE ABOUT THE AUTHOR

Joan Didion was born in California and lives in
New York. She is the author of five novels and six
previous books of nonfiction.

A NOTE ON THE TYPE

The text of this book was set in Garamond No. 3.
It is not a true copy of any of the designs of Claude
Garamond (c. 1480–1561), but an adaptation of his
types, which set the European standard for two centuries. This particular version is based on an adaptation by Morris Fuller Benton.

Composed by Stratford Publishing Services,
Brattleboro, Vermont

Printed and bound by R. R. Donnelley & Sons,
Harrisonburg, Virginia